BATTLE LINES

BATTLE LINES

Report of the
Twentieth Century Fund
Task Force on the Military
and the Media

Background Paper
by Peter Braestrup

 Priority Press Publications/New York/1985

The Twentieth Century Fund is an independent research foundation which undertakes policy studies of economic, political, and social institutions and issues. The Fund was founded in 1919 and endowed by Edward A. Filene.

Copyright © 1985 by the Twentieth Century Fund, Inc.
Manufactured in the United States of America.
ISBN: 0-87078-165-0

FOREWORD

O UR LAST really patriotic war was World War II, when following Pearl Harbor public opinion and the press rallied behind the nation's armed forces, which of course were made up overwhelmingly of citizens rather than professional soldiers. On occasion, the press expressed criticisms of military leaders and tactics, but by and large, trust and cooperation prevailed. The nature of warfare has changed over the past forty years and, to a considerable extent, so has the nature of reporting it. These changes have exacerbated, perhaps to a dangerous point, the healthy tensions that have always existed between the military and the media, as exemplified in the charges and countercharges that have attended incidents in Lebanon, Central America, and on Grenada.

In all likelihood, we will never again see a protracted yet patriotic conflict such as World War II; instead, we may face either the unthinkable—a nuclear holocaust—or small brushfire wars that are unlikely to generate widespread support. These changes led the Trustees of the Twentieth Century Fund to sanction the establishment of an independent Task Force to consider what can be done to prevent relations between the military and the press from becoming so strained as to restrict the flow of information to the American public during military engagements. It was encouraging that the military itself showed concern about this problem in the aftermath of Grenada, where the media had initially been kept from accompanying our troops.

But the Fund did not think that the report of the Sidle panel, though useful in dealing with logistics for adequate press coverage, treated the underlying problems involved in military-media relations. For its part, the Task Force, made up of media and military representatives as well as a number of authorities with experience in government service and in politics, focused on the critical role of civilian authorities, which is the key to seeing to it that the different needs of the military and the media are accommodated.

The Task Force has performed a valuable service not only in its recommendations, which are directed mainly at the civilians in control of the Pentagon and the White House, but also in giving short shrift to a number of concerns that it considered exaggerated. In its deliberations, it found that widely expressed fears about the sheer size of the press corps, or the presence of offbeat or free-lance reporters claiming to represent fringe publications or electronic outlets, or the marvels of technology such as coverage of combat situations as they take place via satellite do not call for increased restrictions on the media. On the contrary, they can be handled by effective planning.

It is the Task Force's considered view that the media and the military can resolve their problems, especially at the front where they face common confusions and common dangers. Most of the caustic press criticism of the Vietnam War did not come from the field but from Washington, where relations were probably as strained between the military and the civilian leadership as between the military and the media. So if there is to be more effective press coverage of our military, it is more the responsibility of the civilian authorities than the military or the press.

The Task Force had the benefit of hearing a number of guest witnesses in the course of its works. On behalf of the Fund as well as the Task Force, I want to express our thanks to the following individuals who made presentations and responded to questions:

Keyes Beech, former war correspondent in Korea and Vietnam for *The Chicago Daily News* and a member of the Sidle panel; Commodore Jack Garrow, chief of public affairs for the U.S. Navy; Benno Schmidt, dean of the Columbia Law School; Diane Zimmerman, professor of law at New York University and former reporter for *Newsweek* and the New York *Daily News;* Michael I. Burch, assistant secretary of defense for public affairs; General Bruce Palmer, Jr., former vice chief of staff for the U.S. Army; Tom Ross, assistant secretary of defense for public affairs in the Carter administration; Stephen Rosenfeld, deputy editorial page editor of *The Washington Post;* Frances Fitzgerald, author of *Fire in the Lake;* Drew Middleton, former military correspondent for *The New York Times;* Marlene Sanders, correspondent, CBS News; Jane Wallace, correspondent, CBS News; Bernard Diederich, correspondent for *Time* magazine.

Most of all, though, I am grateful to the members of the Task Force; its chairman, Edward Costikyan; and its rapporteur, Peter Braestrup, who wrote the informative background paper that accompanies the Report. All of them participated in an independent capacity and all gave freely of their time and experience, making what I believe is a valuable contribution to the future of military-media relations. We are in their debt.

M. J. Rossant, DIRECTOR
The Twentieth Century Fund
May 1985

CONTENTS

TASK FORCE MEMBERS

Edward N. Costikyan, *chairman*
Partner, Paul, Weiss, Rifkind, Wharton & Garrison, New York

Charles Corddry
Defense Correspondent, the *Baltimore Sun*

Shelby Foote
Author, South Memphis, Tennessee

Edward M. Fouhy
Executive Producer, NBC Network News, Washington, D.C.

Jerry Friedheim
Executive Vice President, American Newspaper Publishers Association, Reston, Virginia

Roswell Gilpatric
Partner, Cravath, Swaine & Moore, New York; former Deputy Secretary of Defense

Charlayne Hunter-Gault
National Correspondent, MacNeil-Lehrer News Hour, New York

Samuel P. Huntington
Eaton Professor of the Science of Government and Director, Center for International Affairs, Harvard University

Robert Murray
Lecturer in Public Policy and Director of National Security Programs, John F. Kennedy School of Government, Harvard University

Colonel Harry G. Summers, Jr.
General Douglas MacArthur Chair of Military Research, Army War College, Carlisle Barracks, Pennsylvania

Craig R. Whitney
Assistant Managing Editor, *The New York Times*

Admiral Elmo Zumwalt
President, Admiral Zumwalt and Associates, Inc., Arlington, Virginia; former Chief of Naval Operations and member of the Joint Chiefs of Staff

Peter Braestrup, *rapporteur*
Editor, *Wilson Quarterly*

REPORT OF THE TASK FORCE

I N OCTOBER 1983, when U.S. forces invaded Grenada, American journalists were deliberately barred. They were kept away not only during the brief, two-battalion assault phase, but for two days thereafter. Even when a small group was finally admitted, it was clear that the U.S. government had failed to plan adequately for a flow of information via print and broadcast from Grenada to the American public.

Fortunately, the Grenada operation achieved its objectives quickly. But the government's failure, at the outset, to allow an independent flow of information to the public about a major military operation was unprecedented in modern American history. It provoked fresh arguments over relations between the military and the media, with their sometimes conflicting goals of defending the nation and informing the citizenry; the role of the civilian government in setting information policy in war zones; the responsibilities of journalists in wartime; and the influence of television on the nation's will to apply military force in support of foreign policy. It also highlighted the continuing, deep hostility among many in the military toward the news media, especially toward television.

This Task Force, convened in late 1984, sought to explore the nature of these conflicts and to recommend remedies for this potentially damaging breakdown in relations. We started with the premise that U.S. information policy in a war zone is a civilian concern, not simply a military operational one. Prior to 1983, U.S. presidents understood that they bore this responsibility; they did not relinquish it to military commanders.

In World War II, Korea, Vietnam, and lesser military engagements, civilian authorities saw to it that, in keeping with our tradition as an open society, reasonable provision was made for journalists in war zones. There was tacit agreement between the military and the media that the president, in his role as commander-in-chief, and his civilian subordinates assumed responsibility for media policy as for the war effort as a whole. Civilian authority did not defer, as it did in Grenada, to the commander in the field.

It is critical, in wartime as well as in peacetime, that our democracy have the freest possible flow of information. *Accordingly, the Task Force*

3

believes that the presence of journalists in war zones is not a luxury but a necessity. Imperfect though it is, our independent press serves as the vital link between the battlefield and the home front, reporting on the military's successes, failures, and sacrifices. By doing so, the media have helped to foster citizen involvement and support, which presidents, admirals, and generals have recognized as essential to military success.

This Task Force does not think that it is the mission of the press to mobilize public opinion for war. To the contrary, it is the chief executive who must define the purposes of the nation's use of force and enlist the support of the public and Congress for military action. If an administration's war policy is marked by debate at home, that debate will be reflected and reported in the press, as it was most recently during the conflicts in Korea and Vietnam.

For reasons of security, the media have always accepted restraints on the publication of news, ranging from embargoes and "ground rules," voluntarily adhered to by journalists, to outright military censorship on the battlefield. From the Normandy landings in 1944 to the defense of Khe Sanh in South Vietnam in 1968, practicality has often limited the number of journalists who could be accommodated by individual units or on specific operations. But coverage of such operations established, without challenge, the principle that the press ought to be on hand and helped to report as freely as possible on what was—and was not—happening in the war zone.

Acceptance of this principle could not ensure that the public was well informed. It did not guarantee competence on the part of journalists or news organizations, or candor and adequate knowledge on the part of every military spokesman. The fog of war and the inherent limitations of journalism often blurred the running portrait of battle. Yet, application of the principle meant that on all but a few occasions, the government, the military, and the public were well served.

This traditional arrangement between the press and government was disrupted by the deliberate exclusion from Grenada of *all* reporters during the first two days of the operation and then by the government's failure to plan for the timely accommodation of journalists. *The Task Force believes that this breach need not have occurred, and that no valid security reason existed for excluding all reporters from the immediate post-assault phase.* At the policy direction of the president or the secretary of defense, and with routine planning by the military, a small pool of journalists can always be selected and taken along, with reasonable notice, on a major operation.

The initial reaction among news organizations following the Grenada exclusion featured some excessively self-righteous rhetoric. The response from some military officers and civilians in the Pentagon was not flavored by admiration for the virtues of a free press. But before the debate subsided it brought to the surface some important considerations, including a widening "culture gap" that was, if anything, particularly pronounced between young military officers and reporters. Yet the debate also had a bright side. It provided an opportunity for all sides to take stock of their attitudes and of their professional procedures, and to assess their readiness to provide the public with accurate, comprehensive reporting of any future American involvement in combat.

Civilian Supremacy

In the aftermath of Grenada, an official attempt was made to set up new operational procedures for accommodating the media. But a critical point about that attempt has been overlooked by most observers: the government's effort was initiated, not by the White House or by the Pentagon's *civilian* authorities, but by General John W. Vessey, Jr., the chairman of the Joint Chiefs of Staff. It was Vessey, rather than the president or the secretary of defense, who appointed Winant Sidle, a retired army major general, to convene a panel of military officers and retired journalists to suggest workable arrangements for accommodating the press in battle. Although spokesmen for news organizations testified before the panel, they did not serve on it because they considered serving on a government body inappropriate.

With memories of Grenada still fresh, the Sidle panel naturally devoted much of its attention to those cases where only a small number of journalists could be accommodated in the early stages of combat. In such emergencies, it suggested, media pools should be formed, and it recommended that such pools be impartial and as widely representative of the press as possible (see Appendix).

The Task Force commends the Sidle panel for its unswerving belief that reporters should have the fullest possible access to the battlefield consistent with troop safety and mission security. The Pentagon's first attempt, in late April, to test the pool arrangement recommended by the panel demonstrated the need for patient, detailed preparations for such exercises. The test entailed secretly flying a group of reporters to a military exercise in Honduras on short notice. When word about the exercise leaked, some in the military wondered whether reporters could be entrusted with sensitive assignments. The members of this Task Force firmly believe that the real lesson to be learned was that such procedures must be painstakingly honed in peacetime if they are to function effectively in moments of crisis.

Although we endorse the Sidle panel's recommendations, we think that the White House or the civilian authorities in the Pentagon ought to have established the panel. *The Task Force believes that just as the president and his civilian deputies bear the responsibility for prosecuting a war, so must they assume responsibility for policy decisions on press access and censorship.*

The secretary of defense has taken the welcome step of assembling his own advisory group of veteran journalists, but he has yet to give unequivocal support to the notion that information policy is a civilian responsibility and not one that can be delegated, as it was during the Grenada invasion, to military commanders. Everyone agrees that the safety of troops should not be jeopardized, but, as in past conflicts, the attitude of those in charge should be that reporters ought to be there. The basic question to be posed is: "How can we get them in?" not "How can we keep them out?"

The Question of Access

The public's need for timely information about its government's military operations is implicit in the constitutional guarantees that underpin our society, including the First Amendment. But the question of the right of access by journalists to war zones has been clouded by legal ambiguity; it may, or may not, be enforceable in a court of law.* In any event, *the Task Force believes that it is healthier for the press and for our democratic polity if such complicated constitutional issues are not left to the courts.* Precise legal determinations of press rights in combat could be contentious and might end up limiting press freedoms in the effort to preserve them. *The Task Force would far prefer to see press access to combat operations arranged, as in the past, through cooperative understandings between government and news media.* We also believe that if an administration in the future seeks to bar news media from reasonable access to U.S. combat operations, *the Congress should exert its influence to guarantee a speedy restoration of the historic understanding between the military and the media.*

Samuel P. Huntington dissents: I fully believe the government should support and assist media coverage of military operations for the reason, well stated elsewhere in the report, that both the public and decisionmakers should have an independent source of information. To achieve this end, it is unnecessary to invoke a mythical "right of access." The First Amendment protects the right to speak and publish; it provides no right of access to anything. In addition, the rights protected by the First Amendment are not limited to any class of people. The First Amendment could not give a right of access to military operations to journalists without giving it to all Americans—which it obviously does not.

The Political Context of Military Intervention

To some degree, the reluctance of military commanders to accommodate the media in Grenada might have come about because of the strict controls on the British press during coverage of the Falklands War. Perhaps even more, it reflects a lingering nostalgia for the halcyon days of World War II. Although that war was not without its tensions between the military and the press, it is remembered by many as a time of patriotic harmony when the press, at home and abroad, was "on the team." Yet short of a war for national survival, it is unlikely that future wars will command such universal public support, nor is it likely that we will see another protracted global conflict. Rather, it is probable that when it comes to military strategy and operations, we will witness what has prevailed ever since the founding of the Republic: Americans at odds. Limited regional wars and guerrilla conflicts do not inspire unanimous support.

The probable regional character of future conflicts also means that U.S. combat forces may again be deployed in countries where host governments are hostile to foreign journalists. In such cases, the U.S. government should make vigorous diplomatic efforts to ensure, at a minimum, the access of American reporters to American forces. Public support for "secret" U.S. military operations, or inadequately reported ones, will not long endure.

Planning for the Press

Because public affairs planning should not be improvised in the heat of battle, the Task Force recommends that a "public affairs annex" be considered a routine feature in all plans for U.S. military operations. Included in the planning should be measures to assist and accredit journalists; procedures for embargoes, "guidelines," and other legitimate restraints on the type and timing of information that can be reported; and provision for special "pools" of journalists to accompany U.S. forces on surprise missions. (There are many precedents for such pool arrangements in wartime.)

To ensure the maximum flow of information to the public and the government, the Task Force recommends that the secretary of defense reemphasize the importance of Department of Defense public affairs officers, both civilian and military. Senior field commanders should recognize that such officers serve as important conduits, via the news media, to the citizenry and government. They should be treated, by superiors and field officers, as "insiders," participating in the planning of impending military operations and serving as informed spokesmen for the field commander in the war zone. This public affairs role has been recognized and faithfully implemented by leading U.S. commanders—including Dwight D. Eisenhower, Chester Nimitz, Matthew Ridgway, William C. Westmoreland, and Creighton W. Abrams—since the beginning of World War II.

Ground Rules.*

The security of tactical operations is a legitimate military concern, and one that must not be dismissed by journalists. *To preserve the security of U.S. military operations, the Task Force favors the use of clearly stated "ground rules," such as existed in Vietnam.* These guidelines, voluntarily adhered to by journalists and enforced by the field commander, delineate those pieces of information, such as troop movements or unit identification in battle, that could imperil U.S. forces if reported by journalists. We regard a system of ground rules as less cumbersome and more effective than the mandatory, military field censorship used in World War II and Korea, which often led to unnecessary delays in the transmission of news, and required trained field censors and the application of consistent criteria for judging security violations. A censorship system may tempt military officials to invoke the rationale of security to black out news that might simply be embarrassing.

Although civilian authorities should lay down the broad outlines of information policy in combat, the Task Force recommends that the procedural details be left to the commander in the field. When he enforces ground rules, the military commander should, of course, have the firm backing of civilian authority. Those who violate the rules should, if necessary, be subject to sanctions laid down in advance, and all correspondents should be treated consistently and fairly. News organizations should impress upon reporters sent into combat zones the importance of scrupulous adherence to such rules to ensure that their effectiveness is not compromised by journalistic competitiveness or irresponsibility.

---

*Craig R. Whitney comments: If our report is interpreted to express support for restrictive arrangements, I disagree with that interpretation. We should urge the military to be more open and forthright in its information policies, not to enumerate more restrictive measures, such as "pools" and ground rules. Civilian authorities should make it clear to the military chain of command that its duty is not to hedge in correspondents with restraints, but to be as informative as possible. Mutually agreed upon ground rules and sanctions may be necessary in some cases (although not in as many as the military authorities usually think). Our purpose is not to recommend their use, but to state that of the two evils, censorship is worse than restraints on some categories of information.

The military and the executive branch have a corresponding obligation to maintain the integrity of this relationship. The credibility of military operations will erode if journalists and the public believe that deception, secrecy, or press curbs in war zones are being employed, not for security reasons, but to serve the needs of domestic politics or bureaucratic self-protection. The lessons of history are instructive in this regard; on those rare occasions when the executive branch employed military leaders as spokesmen in order to try to manipulate the media and Congress for short-term political advantage, the practice eventually contributed to crises of confidence for both the military establishment and the civilian executive branch.

The Culture Divide

Military-media relations have never been entirely smooth, in part because of the very nature of war, but also in part because of historic differences between the two callings. Now, as in the past, each tends to attract different personality types and to foster different sets of values. Of necessity, military people are schooled to respect tradition, authority, and leadership; obedience is an inescapable part of military life. In contrast, because journalists on occasion have the job of challenging official wisdom, their ranks tend to be filled with those who are more free-wheeling, irreverent, and skeptical of authority. The culture gap is compounded by competing goals. Some tension will always exist between the military's mission of winning on the battlefield and the combat journalist's mission of providing the public with timely information on what is taking place.

As we see it, the divide between the military and the media is in danger of widening. On the media side, the overwhelming majority of young reporters have had no firsthand exposure to combat, let alone to military life or even to those who have had experience of it, in large part due to the end of conscription in 1972, the large-scale avoidance of the draft by college-educated males during Vietnam, and the recent influx of women into journalism. On the military side, younger officers—those under age thirty—also have no firsthand experience of combat, but they have, even though only at secondhand, a store of beliefs absorbed from their elders. Both young and old military people seem to be gripped by powerful myths about the media dating from Vietnam. To some extent, this is a response to critical newspaper reporting from Vietnam and Washington during the war and to the widespread belief that television coverage soured public opinion on the war.

We do not believe that the gap between the two cultures can—or should—be closed, but we recommend that steps be taken to keep what was traditionally a healthy adversarial relationship from deteriorating into antagonism. As the Sidle panel stressed, good planning by the executive branch, including the military services, plus common sense on the part of news organizations, should work to minimize tensions.

News media executives must keep in mind the lack of experience of military life among younger journalists, remembering that many spent their college years on campuses where hostility toward the military was pervasive. *The Task Force therefore recommends that news organizations urge the directors of the mid-career training programs for journalists at a number of major universities, as well as the heads of schools of journalism, to hold seminars and other functions with military people so as to broaden journalists' familiarity with their military counterparts.*

The Task Force also recommends that the Defense Department offer brief, field-familiarization programs to reporters from major news organizations. Their objective should be to allow reporters and news executives to become acquainted with military personnel, organization, tactics, weaponry, and logistics. This, obviously, cannot be done in a day. We also urge that reporters—particularly those likely to be assigned to cover military operations under planned pool arrangements—be invited to attend major military maneuvers of longer duration. Senior news executives should see to it that reporters take advantage of such opportunities.

The Task Force also recommends that the Defense Department encourage greater sophistication among its officers about the First Amendment, the role of a free press in American society, journalistic processes, and the limitations and strengths of American journalism generally. Courses dealing with these issues should be part of the core curriculum at mid- and senior-level service schools, and the occasional media-military seminars at the U.S. Naval War College and its counterparts in other services should be expanded. These courses should discuss the need for a cooperative working relationship between the military and the media and provide a history of the evolution of that relationship.

The Role of the Press

Public opinion polls—and the rising number of adverse jury verdicts in libel cases—suggest that the media do not bask in universal public esteem. Despite the success of individual television news stars in attracting high audience ratings, journalists as a group have seldom—the Watergate era is the major exception—ranked high in popularity. The military seem to focus their dislike of the media on the supposed adverse impact of television on public opinion during military operations. Among the causes of Hanoi's victory in Indochina, many cite what they perceive as the negative impact on home-front morale of television reporting from the battlefield. This perception, which, oddly, has been reinforced by the repeated claims of some network television journalists that powerful pictures alone brought home the brutal "reality" of war, is apparently shared, to a great extent, by the public.

Scholarly data, though, casts some doubt on this view. Although the scenes of actual carnage may be most vividly remembered, they were but a small fraction of the footage from Vietnam. And television was not the only source of the public's perception of the horror of war; there also were widely reproduced photographs that depicted its agony and tragedy. This Task Force also does not believe that television coverage caused the public to lose enthusiasm for the Vietnam War.* Opinion polls have documented that public support for the Vietnam War declined less rapidly than public support for the Korean War, when television coverage was much less significant and military field censorship was in force. The available evidence also suggests that television coverage of Vietnam reflected a critical view of the war only *after* public opinion had begun to oppose it.**

We further note that the televised portrayal of antiwar demonstrations during the Vietnam War, however distressing to public officials, did not seem to rouse the sympathies of the television audience. It is important to remember that, as of 1981, half of the nation's households with television sets did not even watch the network evening news shows. Accordingly, this Task Force urges both the critics and champions of television's alleged role in Vietnam to take a closer look at the evidence and to forego mythology in discussing future military-media arrangements.

Television is not, per se, a threat to the security of U.S. military operations. Potential problems with live transmission of videotape that might pose a hazard to U.S. combat forces can be resolved through mutual

---

Craig R. Whitney dissents: I think it is beyond the scope of our panel to determine in a few paragraphs what it was that caused the American public to turn away from support of the Vietnam War. It is enough to note that many in the military, and in the general public, dislike and distrust the media, and to urge that the media not ignore this state of affairs.

**Samuel P. Huntington dissents:* In reviewing effects of specific coverage, evidence can be found of major shifts in public opinion due to coverage. In January 1968, before the Tet offensive, 56 percent of the public identified themselves as hawks, 28 percent as doves; in March, after Tet, 41 percent identified themselves as hawks, 42 percent as doves. The erroneous media interpretation of Tet as a military disaster must have played a significant role in this shift. See S. Robert Lichter and Stanley Rothman, "The Media and National Defense," in Robert L. Pfaltzgraff, Jr., and Uri Ra'anan, eds., *National Security Policy: The Decision-making Process* (Archon Books, 1984).

Robert Murray and Admiral Elmo Zumwalt join in this dissent.

agreements. So can arrangements for pooling and transporting television crews. The field commander must be the final arbiter of what constitutes a threat to the security of his operations. Advised by civilian authorities and guided by his public affairs officer, he must decide when and how to accommodate television camera crews. In the heat and confusion of battle, words—spoken and written—are often the most efficient means of communicating complex information to the public; pictures are, of course, a useful adjunct.*

We strongly recommend that the media not ignore the current popular resentments and suspicions reflected in the attitude of many military people. Most journalists will readily concede that the major print and broadcast news organizations are not without sin. Their highly competitive managers and reporters do not seek to aid the enemy in wartime, but they are sometimes guilty of hasty judgments, political biases of various shades, a taste for melodrama and misdeeds, selective memory, sloppiness with facts, unfairness, slipshod editing, and lazy thinking.** When it comes to reporting on combat operations, which are inherently difficult to cover, any one of these sins can lead to serious distortions. As in past wars, this happened in Vietnam. But it is worth remembering that in Vietnam, military spokesmen can recall only a handful of *security* violations among the hundreds of accredited journalists in Saigon.

Many critics of the news media, including military men, have called for a more "responsible" press. Yet they are unable to agree on a definition of responsible or on how to enforce responsibility without destroying media independence under the First Amendment. We see responsibility as consisting, first, of news organizations assigning people with knowledge of military affairs to cover combat, and second, of their insisting on reporting and editing that are as fair, accurate, sophisticated, and comprehensive as battlefield circumstances permit. News executives

---

Charlayne Hunter-Gault dissents: This passage seems to suggest acceptance of a different standard for television journalists than for print—to wit, if there are only three seats on the plane, the priority is print, and then the field commander can do whatever he wishes with the television people. Even if you don't buy that old chestnut that "A picture is worth a thousand words," to say that a picture is merely "a useful adjunct" seems to me at least arguable, and in this context certainly an unnecessarily provocative assertion.

**Craig R. Whitney dissents:* It is unfair to catalog the sins of reporters without also noting that military officials have not been free of prejudice, have been selective of the facts, and have revealed personal animosity in their view of the media. In few cases have any of the "sins" listed led to breaches of operational security in past wars—the reason given, in Grenada, for excluding the press.

should realize that their organizations' credibility will suffer unless they assign to combat operations journalists whose skills are commensurate with the complexity and seriousness of their task. *In addition, we believe that a diversity of news media coverage, along with more vigorous media self-scrutiny, are the public's best protection against journalistic sins.*

Conclusion

Thus, we believe that the president must be prepared to make the political effort—and, if necessary, pay the political price—to mobilize public opinion behind any military operation he authorizes. The press and television cannot repair inept leadership or flawed strategy, nor is it their business to try to do so. They cannot win or lose wars or attempt to remake the history they report.

The news media have, on occasion, been guilty of losing perspective on events. In their restless way, they signal first one development in foreign affairs, then another, usually following the public commentary of presidents and their critics. Nevertheless, our free press, when it accompanies the nation's soldiers into battle, performs a unique role. It serves as eyewitness; it forges a bond between the citizen and the soldier; and, at its best, it strives to avoid manipulation either by officials or by critics of the government through accurate, independent reporting. It also provides one of the checks and balances that sustains the confidence of the American people in their political system and armed forces.

Grenada raised the issue of media access to U.S. forces in combat. If we learn the lessons of Grenada, putting the hurly-burly of the battle and the exclusion of the press behind us, we should be able to restore the cooperative attitude that has marked military-media relations in the past. All of us have a stake in seeing to it that the nation's civilian authorities, military leaders, and journalists restore a workable yet arm's-length relationship. It is the best way to ensure a free and informed society.

BACKGROUND PAPER

by Peter Braestrup

PREFACE

T HIS background paper is intended to provide an overview of U.S. military-media relations in overseas battle zones since 1941. For purposes of comparison, the United Kingdom's 1982 War for the Falklands is examined. As an aid to discussion of their respective roles in advancing the public interest, the contrasting "cultures" of the military and of American print and broadcast journalism are also examined.

My objective was to assist the members of a distinguished Twentieth Century Fund Task Force, assembled by M. J. Rossant, director of the Fund, in assessing past American experience and formulating recommendations for resolving the issues that arose in the controversy that followed the exclusion of the news media from Grenada for forty-eight hours after the United States' invasion of that island republic in October 1983.

The sources for this background paper are indicated in the footnotes. It should be emphasized that, while memoirs by generals and war correspondents abound, comprehensive studies of American military-media relations or of war reporting during the conflicts of the 1941-85 period do not yet exist. There are no accounts comparable to those of military-press relations and press performance that were compiled by scholars of the Civil War, the Spanish-American War, and World War I. Much relevant archival material remains to be explored. Of necessity, some of my judgments of military-media relations prior to the Vietnam conflict are tentative.

Overall, I might add, the strengths and weaknesses of American press performance do not seem to have altered much since World War II, even as journalistic themes, reflecting the political environment at home, have changed over time in each case where newspeople accompanied U.S. forces into combat. Television news, on the other hand, has emerged as a distinct art form with special preoccupations of its own.

Leona Hiraoka, an editor of the *Wilson Quarterly,* did the research and first-draft writing for that portion of chapter 7 dealing with the public discussion that followed Grenada. She also supervised the research and fact-checking for the entire manuscript and served as the project's able general manager.

I am indebted to Mark Thompson, a law school graduate and former member of the *Wilson Quarterly* editorial staff, for researching and writing the first draft of that portion of chapter 7 dealing with the Constitutional issues that arose, or seemed to have arisen, in the government-press controversy after Grenada. Mr. Thompson also unearthed original archival material concerning allied plans for press coverage prior to the Normandy landings during World War II.

Given the uneven quality of available documentary sources, I am particularly grateful to the Task Force members and to the following individuals for their guidance, corrective comments, and other assistance:

Keyes Beech, Maj. Donald Black (USAF), Michael Burch, Paul Cassell, Bernard Diederich, Col. James Elmer (USAF), Maj. Douglas Frey (USA), Sandy Gilmour, Howard Handleman, Tom Lambert, S. Robert Lichter, Drew Middleton, Maj. Gen. John E. Murray (USA, ret.), Col. Robert O'Brien (USAF), Bill Plante, Capt. Owen Resweber (USN), Tom Ricks, Robert Sherrod, Maj. Gen. Winant Sidle (USA, ret.), Comm. Ronald Wildermuth (USN), Maj. Barry Willey (USA), Harry Zubkoff.

The paper's sins of omission and commission must be blamed solely on the author.

· 1 ·

INTRODUCTION

BY MOST measures, the United States' hastily planned invasion of Grenada on October 25, 1983, was successful. Cuban and Grenadian resistance was short-lived; several hundred possibly imperiled American medical students were rescued; despite some costly mishaps, casualties were low; and the demise of General Bernard Coard's chaotic, newly installed local revolutionary regime was greeted with more joy than sorrow by the island's 100,000 inhabitants.

But many of the nation's editorial writers and television pundits did not rejoice. Almost as soon as the hostilities on the island died down, those that had arisen between the Reagan administration and the country's major news organizations, particularly those in television, over the exclusion by the military of journalists from the island during the first two days of the invasion erupted into a cold war.

The senior military commanders, with the approval of the White House, had decided to exclude the press and the television cameras from the island not just during the initial assault phase but until the medical students were rescued and well after the worst fighting was over. For forty-eight hours the island was off-limits to newsmen; a few who had gotten ashore in spite of the ban were, in effect, barred from filing their stories. No "pools" of newsmen were organized or transported to the scene.

Not until late on October 27, two days after the landing, after vociferous protests from journalists, were fifteen photographers and reporters brought by air force transports from Barbados (where more than 300 journalists had assembled) for a hasty, guided tour of the Point Salines airfield; over the next three days, more guided tours followed. It was not until October 30 that all restrictions on the press were lifted.

Meanwhile, the earliest "facts" the public received were supplied by ham radio operators in touch with Americans on the island and by intermittent, fragmentary briefings from the Pentagon, then by rescued U.S. medical students, and to some degree by reports from Havana and other Caribbean islands. For almost a week, a multitude of official sources (informed, semi-informed, and uninformed) in Washington were talking about Grenada. Contradictions, rumors, exaggerations (notably of Cuban strength and ferocity) abounded—to be sorted out only later.

The unprecedented administration effort at news management quickly drew fire from senior journalists. "I'm outraged," said Howard Simons, *The Washington Post*'s managing editor.[1] "Intolerable," said Jerry Friedheim, former Pentagon spokesman and executive vice president of the American Newspaper Publishers Association.[2] NBC's John Chancellor said, "The Reagan Administration has produced a bureaucrat's dream: Do anything, no one is watching."[3]

Judging by opinion polls, the public initially did not share the media's outrage. According to a *Los Angeles Times* poll taken from November 12 to 17, 1983, a majority of Americans supported, or at least condoned, the White House decision to exclude journalists during the Grenada military operation. But the same respondents, by a two-to-one margin, opposed making the Grenada news blackout a precedent for future U.S. combat operations.[4]

To the public, spokesmen for major news groups either claimed that the First Amendment gave newsmen right of access to the battlefield or cited tradition, invoking (flawed) memories of past accommodations by the U.S. military to the needs of journalists who in turn provided independent witness to the deeds of America's sons on the battlefield. Newsmen, they said, had always been on hand—from Bull Run to the Normandy beaches, and from Korea to the Dominican Republic and Vietnam.

One aspect of the problem that was not recognized, at least not publicly, by most news executives during the post-Grenada discussion was the fact that in the wake of the Indochinese War and the turbulent 1970s many of the nation's senior military officers, veterans of Vietnam, had developed a bitter consensus: newsmen, especially television newsmen, were, at bottom, adversaries, neither trustworthy nor competent in military affairs, eager to dramatize American failings, possessing enormous power to undercut civilian backing for the men in battle. Some military commentators, as we shall see, went so far as to blame the loss of the Vietnam War on the impact on the home front of television news coverage. The very presence of such adversaries was enough to impose a burden on U.S. commanders in the field, they believed, a burden that was unacceptable in hasty, small-scale expeditions such as that to Grenada. As they saw it, the tight rein kept on the reporters taken along during the 1982 Falklands War by the British was closer to the right idea.

Secretary of State George Shultz, a former marine, did not contest this sentiment: "These days," he told reporters, "in the adversary journalism that's been developed, it seems as though the reporters always are against us. And when you are trying to conduct a military operation, you don't need that."[5] And John E. Murray, a retired army major general and Vietnam veteran, observed in *The Wall Street Journal* that "engaging the press while engaging the enemy is taking on one adversary too many."[6]

Long after the initial furor, Vice Admiral Joseph W. Metcalf III, the commander of the Grenada expedition, conceded that, in terms of logistics and space, he could have accommodated a pool of eight newsmen aboard his flagship, the *Guam*. However, he said, "I did not want the press around where I would start second-guessing what I was doing relative to [what] the press [might choose to report to the public]."[7]

Although Admiral Metcalf was convinced that he and his superiors had been right in barring the news media, Defense Secretary Caspar Weinberger felt that some fence-mending was necessary. By order of General John W. Vessey, Jr., chairman of the Joint Chiefs of Staff, a panel of former journalists and military officers was convened by Winant Sidle, a retired army major general and former military spokesman in Vietnam, to recommend ways of improving military-media relations in future conflicts. The major news organizations agreed to testify before the Sidle panel (but not to join it), and some answered questionnaires sent them by the panel, which was seeking expressions of media wants and needs.

The post-Grenada discussions have clarified some major issues in media-military relationships that needed to be addressed, although it is clear that the issue, at bottom, is one of mutual trust and comprehension.

The Past. To a degree, both the suspicions of the military and the claims of newspeople are based on flawed recollections, bordering on myth, of American media-military relations—and media performance—in various combat zones over the past four decades. Reexamining this history will allow the discussions of the role of each to be based on something close to historical truth rather than selective memory.

Autonomy. In the wake of Vietnam and Watergate, a substantial number of news executives have come to contend that, in the public interest and under the First Amendment, the nation's news organizations should be seen as a kind of fourth branch of government, an autonomous watchdog over other major institutions. But does this mean that the growing claims of special privilege for journalists—pressed in cases involving access to court proceedings, governmental records, and penal institutions—should be extended to U.S. military operations in combat zones as well?

Roone Arledge, president of ABC News, noted, by way of analogy, that "conflicts . . . arise between the First Amendment right of a free press and the Sixth Amendment guarantee of a free trial as it is now interpreted. . . . Nobody has yet decided how to solve it . . . it simply exists. . . ."

"Our society," he suggested, "may be best served when government and press understand that each performs separate and ultimately autonomous functions. . . ."[8]

Military commanders in future combat operations, however, are unlikely to share that view. When men's lives are at stake, when public perceptions (and political leaders' perceptions) of the battlefield are in part shaped by the news media, the notion of accommodating a profession that considers itself autonomous and by implication "neutral" or "critical" even in wartime is unlikely to appeal to generals, their civilian superiors, or the combat troops.

Censorship. The claim of autonomy also has cropped up in discussions of future military censorship of television film and press dispatches. After Grenada, Jack Foisie, the veteran *Los Angeles Times* war correspondent, argued that a "degree of censorship always is acceptable in wartime, even preferred. It shifts the judgment for 'not endangering lives' to military professionals; it gives all correspondents an even start in this competitive business; and it makes troop commanders a lot more ready to talk candidly."[9]

But the notion of censorship in combat zones was new to a few spokesmen in Washington for several major news organizations; in the last big war, in Vietnam, there was no censorship, just as there was none in Grenada. "Under no circumstances," said William W. Headline, bureau chief for Cable News Network, voicing a minority view, "could we acquiesce in direct censorship of our reports as a *precondition* to coverage of military operations. . . . Coverage, if censored, would be likely to have harmful effects on the credibility of the Defense Department . . . as well as on media which might convey such coverage."[10]

Constraints. The issue of barring the press and television for foreign policy reasons also emerged in the response of media organizations to the Sidle panel's query: What should the U.S. government do if the government of a host country to which U.S. forces were deployed insisted on banning reporters? (The Sidle panel had in mind the Persian Gulf area.) Said the National Association of Broadcasters:

> The presence of U.S. newspersons should be a *precondition* to granting U.S. military aid. . . . Realistically, countries in dire need of U.S. military aid are not likely to forego assistance in order to keep U.S. journalists out.[11] [emphasis added]

In fact, as several military men noted, America's allies have put some curbs, if not outright bans, on U.S. journalists in the past. During the Vietnam War, for example, Thailand, a member of the Southeast Asia Treaty Organization, played host to five major U.S. Air Force bases from which came most of the air force strikes against North Vietnam; preferring a low profile, the Thais successfully insisted that the bases be under nominal Thai command and that American journalists not openly visit the bases without Thai permission. (In practice, U.S. journalists interviewed air force people "off-base," or did not disclose in their reporting that they had been "on-base.") Similar curbs might be likely in the Persian Gulf and the Caribbean should U.S. forces go into action there.

Access to the "Other Side." By implication, the question of "autonomy" raised the issue of unrestrained access by American journalists to "the other side." During the Korean War, only Western Communists, notably Australia's Wilfred Burchett, visited the enemy camp. Travel by Americans to North Korea (and China) was forbidden by the State Department, and no one who sought to challenge this rule was admitted by North Korea.

In El Salvador, where Communist-backed guerrillas are engaged in combat against an army trained and advised by the United States, there has been no retaliation by the U.S. government against American newsmen who visited the guerrillas. Nor has there been any U.S. attempt to bar American newsmen from reporting from Nicaragua—where the United States maintains an embassy and the Central Intelligence Agency (C.I.A.) supports the antigovernment "contra" guerrillas. In October 1983, while Cubans and Americans were in combat in Grenada, there was no official U.S. inhibition on American journalists accepting invitations to Havana.

During the Vietnam War, where U.S. troops were directly involved, neither Lyndon Johnson nor Richard Nixon put Hanoi off-limits to any U.S. journalist (or antiwar activist) who could persuade the North Vietnamese to let him in. Harrison Salisbury's vivid, sympathetic dispatches from Hanoi in *The New York Times* in 1966, stemming from a guided tour of urban damage due to U.S. bombing raids, were one result still deplored by U.S. military men. Next time, it has been said, the foe should not have a pipeline to the U.S. public. In wartime, should the U.S. press—or other Americans—be banned from travel to the "other side"?

Accommodating Technology. As yet dimly understood, there are problems involved in accommodating the increased requirements of television news (the demands of complex television technology mean that more manpower, transport, communications, and satellite up-links will be needed) in the combat zone. This will be a bigger problem when U.S. forces consist of widely dispersed "austere" and rapidly shifting units, as is likely to be the case in Central America and the Persian Gulf and as was the case in Grenada. At one point, there were more than 300 journalists in Barbados waiting to go to Grenada; perhaps one-third of them were involved in some way with television; ABC News alone had twenty-five people on the scene, more than the entire U.S. press contingent that actually landed with U.S. forces on the beaches of Normandy on June 6, 1944.

If we assume that the goal of senior military men and their civilian superiors is making the maximum amount of information available to the U.S. public, what set of priorities, if any, should the U.S. military adopt with respect to the various media—wire services, newspapers, newsmagazines, television networks, radio?

Mutual Comprehension. Since World War II, the two cultures—the military and the media—have rarely been so divided. The fact that a high proportion of college-age males escaped service during the Vietnam War, the end of the draft in 1972, and the influx of women into journalism all mean that an increasing proportion of editors and television producers, to say nothing of young reporters, have had no direct exposure to the military. For their part, in an odd way, many senior military men have come to regard the "media" as all of a piece, and television news as synonymous with "the media," although print organizations and television are very different institutions, operating under very different pressures and requirements.

As has been clear from the outset, the underlying problem is one of mutual comprehension and trust. The fact is that since 1941, under many trying circumstances, the military and the media have managed to accommodate each other, often in surprising ways, mostly without undue jeopardy to either military operations or the healthy flow of information to the U.S. public. This said, history also shows us that all was not in harmony during World War II, that newsmen *sought* military censorship during the Korean War, that reporters did not *expect* instant access during the 1965 Dominican intervention, that journalists enjoyed unusual freedom and facilities during the Vietnam conflict, and that the British, out of necessity, curbed (but did not exclude) newsmen during the 1982 Falklands expedition. If nothing else, the Grenada affair showed what happens when the military does *not* make plans to accommodate the media and when the media concentrate on their own problems instead of following up on the events on the ground. We still do not have a comprehensive postmortem by newsmen of the Grenada military operation itself, and we still have a trickle of revelations, false, true, or half-true, about the U.S. military's performance on the island.

The past should not be used to draw up a set of hard rules to fit every possible contingency in the future. But since it is likely that the United States will be involved in combat overseas, short of a superpower conflict, again in this century, the government and the media need to ponder and discuss their relationship and their mutual Constitutional responsibilities to a free society. They need to take note of their respective roles—to gain military success at the lowest cost and to keep the public adequately informed about the sacrifices and successes of its sons on the battlefield. A brief look at the past may help the discussion.

· 2 ·

WORLD WAR II

HE Japanese attack on Pearl Harbor created a rare unity among Americans. It ended two years of bitter debate, now largely forgotten, in Congress, the press, and on the nation's college campuses over Franklin D. Roosevelt's increasingly overt policy of rearmament and aid to the Allies against the advancing Axis powers. It also generated a major expansion of coverage by the nation's newspapers and a common understanding by press and government that the freest possible reporting would sustain public support for the war effort. World War II, of course, spurred the greatest military effort by the United States in its history, eventually putting 11.9 million American troops overseas in Europe, Africa, the Persian Gulf, India, Burma, China, Australia, and the Pacific, with the navy and army air forces everywhere engaged.

In contrast to the thirty-eight reporters accredited to the headquarters of General John J. Pershing's American Expeditionary Force in France in 1917-18, American newsmen were allowed easy access to the battlefield in 1941-45.[1] Although subject to censorship, like their World War I counterparts, they were usually allowed to go where they wished, often with a public affairs officer as expediter and escort.

Contrary to current mythology, however, the U.S. press and radio did not go *everywhere*—there were not enough reporters to cover every battle on land, sea, or in the air. The role of the Allies often got short shrift, especially in Asia and the Pacific. And even eyewitness reports of Americans were delayed by communications difficulties.

Many—perhaps most—of the war's major actions were, initially at least, reported from rear-echelon headquarters—including the massive D-Day landings of June 6, 1944, in Normandy, when only a handful of reporters went ashore. And no reporters were present at some major battles, notably the successful defense of encircled Bastogne by Major General Anthony McAuliffe's 101st Airborne Division during the Germans' last ditch Ardennes offensive ("The Battle of the Bulge") in December 1944. Moreover, as was to happen again in Korea and Vietnam, newsmen, with few exceptions, did not stay with the same units week after week, or deploy systematically to cover all aspects of a given campaign. As always, newsmen were competitors, not a collective. Based at or near a military headquarters (source of communications, transport, and some version of a Big Picture), each reporter picked the most likely "story" in the field and sought it out, returning to file or broadcast.[2]

Much excellent daily journalism resulted, but there was plenty of information left over for magazine writers and historians. The sheer scale and variety of worldwide U.S. operations, to say nothing of Allied operations, were beyond the capacity of journalists to capture in anything approaching a "first rough draft of history." Yet, in the main, the critical events were covered, at least in *The New York Times* and other major newspapers. Americans were not left in the dark as to the war's progress, costs, difficulties, and high-echelon debates. The woes of civilians caught in the fighting were reported—if not emphasized. If soldiers' misdeeds (e.g., the shooting of German prisoners) or the unsurgical bombing of Italian railroads or German cities seldom got into print, there were plenty of articles criticizing strategy or tactics. Reports of the marines' heavy casualties at Tarawa in the Pacific, for example, stirred widespread debate in 1943. Yet newsmen were considered part of the war effort, and, in Washington and overseas, the representatives of most of the prestigious news organizations were taken into the confidence of such senior military leaders as General George Catlett Marshall, U.S. chief of staff, General Douglas MacArthur, and Admiral Chester W. Nimitz. William L. Laurence, science reporter for *The New York Times*, was invited, under vows of silence, to do advance research on the Manhattan Project for five months, so his newspaper could publish *that* story right after the dropping of the A-bombs on Japan in 1945.[3]

The U.S. amphibious landings in the Mediterranean and in the Pacific, necessarily preceded by lengthy planning and voyages aboard troop transports, were good for journalists. Like political conventions at home, they were set-piece affairs. Military commanders and newsmen had time to get to know one another. The journalists had time to understand the problem and the plan—and hence gain some basis for later assessments of what actually took place. One need only read *Tarawa* by Robert Sherrod of *Time* to see how an intelligent reporter could profit by such lengthy prior exposure—and how little of the marines' overall battle on that tiny Pacific island he actually saw during the bloody chaos of D-Day. Like the combatants themselves, he saw little but vignettes; only a few days later could he pull together the chronicle, but it was a chronicle informed by prior self-instruction and by firsthand observation.[4]

Communications, transport, and occasional bouts with censorship preoccupied reporters throughout World War II. Few reporters, contrary to myth, were uncritical of the generals or loath to air feuds among the Allies. But few dwelled on the sufferings of German civilians under Allied bombing or the atrocities inflicted by U.S. troops advancing into Germany. War was war. At the very end, as if to underscore the press's independence, Edward Kennedy of the Associated Press broke an official embargo, set largely for diplomatic and political reasons, on the announcement of Germany's surrender in May 1945; he became a hero to some colleagues, a villain to others (who had abided by the embargo).[5]

Throughout the war, on the home front, the civilian Office of War Information (OWI), headed by radio broadcaster Elmer Davis, supervised propaganda efforts aimed at the neutral and the Axis powers and, by and large, prodded the military to encourage a free flow of information, which was considered essential to civilian support for the war effort. "The view of this official is that everything should be printed if it does not endanger the national security," said Davis.[6] Indeed, on occasion, in late 1944, after the success of Allied forces in France and the western Pacific, the OWI officials issued public warnings against home-front complacency.[7] President Roosevelt appointed Byron Price as director of censorship on December 18, 1941, relieving the FBI of that emergency responsibility, and created the Office of Censorship, with Price as its head. Price worked out a voluntary "Code of Wartime Practices," with the full cooperation of press and broadcast executives, which became effective January 15, 1942. In essence, the code defined the kinds of data (e.g., troop shifts, ship movements) that could not be publicized at home without official authorization and established procedures for clearing information.

But the military services retained authority to censor all dispatches emanating from overseas theaters of war. Initially, the biggest problems came from Admiral Ernest J. King, chief of naval operations, who distrusted the press and sought to delay news of naval defeats in the Pacific beyond any security needs. The navy's heavy-handedness only eased after the intercessions of Elmer Davis and Hanson Baldwin of *The New York Times*.[8]

Some official strictures were placed on photographs: as far as can be ascertained, photos of American battle dead were not published until 1943 when *Life* printed one of a helmeted American GI face down, half-buried in the sand on a New Guinea beach.[9] Thereafter, such photos were rarely published, as were photos of American wounded. Casualty lists were released by the Pentagon on a regular basis.

It is worth noting here that the three major picture agencies—Associated Press, Acme, International News Photos—and *Life* created a photographic war pool under an agreement signed in late January 1942. Under it, they were to pool their resources, supplying photographers for the war fronts from the staffs of all four organizations, whose pictures were then available to all four. (During World War I the armed services' own photographers had taken virtually all the front-line action pictures; in World War II, army, navy, and marine photographers also played a big role but enjoyed no monopoly.) By April 1943, twenty-eight pool photographers were on assignment in every part of the world where the war was being fought, at a combined cost to the pool members of approximately $400,000 a year.[10] The photography pool left the newsreels to their own devices.

Initially, the Army Signal Corps transmitted pool pictures by wire and wireless direct to the United States from North Africa after the invasion there in 1942. Distribution of all pictures was to be on an immediate, simultaneous basis whenever release was made by the army and navy. Pictures were generally censored at the source by staffs under the army or navy commander. Then the pictures were relayed to Washington for another look-see by the War or Navy Department. On the whole, the dispatch to the United States was reasonably prompt, by plane when possible. The bottleneck was in Washington, where the censors held pictures longer than the pool thought necessary while determining what to release.[11]

The military-press relationship was nowhere more exhaustively planned during World War II than in London prior to the Normandy landings on June 6, 1944. After two years of directing military operations, General Dwight D. Eisenhower had learned a good deal from past experience, some of it unhappy, in North Africa and Sicily.[12] Both Eisenhower and his staff at Supreme Headquarters Allied Expeditionary Force (SHAEF), including Army Brigadier General Thomas Jefferson Davis, chief, public relations division, were determined that for the coming Normandy invasion—Operation Overlord—there would be a well-organized system for the support of newspapermen assigned to the Normandy beaches and (mostly) to backup stations. The planning that went into accommodating the press was as extensive as that for any phase of Operation Overlord.[13]

There was much discussion within SHAEF many months before the invasion itself over the problems of dealing with the press. There were consultations among the British Ministry of Information, British military information officers, and the Americans. One of the problems, as set forth in memos, minutes, and other documents now in the National Archives, was the problem of giving several hundred correspondents in London awaiting D-Day enough to write about in February, March, and April of 1944. The preparations for the invasion had to be kept secret, and many parts of England were off-limits to reporters.

One of the questions that arose repeatedly in SHAEF was how much of the buildup for D-Day could be open to newsmen (that is, to provide pictures and descriptions of training, the amassing of supplies, the arrival of new equipment). All of this was tied to the purpose of keeping up home-front morale with the assurance that, in fact, progress was being made or would be made in the war against Hitler.

Internally, there was an agreement between the British and the Americans not to attempt to use the press to deceive the Germans with what is now called "disinformation." As Brigadier General Robert A. McClure, the assistant chief of staff at SHAEF for psychological warfare and public relations, wrote to Sir Cyril Radcliffe of the British Ministry of Information: "Men who profess to present the news honestly should not be subjected to official suasion to present it dishonestly, however laudable the purpose. We cannot remove the foundations of a house and expect it to remain standing."[14]

On April 24, 1944, there was a major conference of American and British military public affairs officers in London. The minutes of that meeting indicate that all present were still concerned with the problem of protecting the security of the D-Day invasion (which involved deceiving the Germans as to where and when the assault would be launched; it was hoped that the Germans could be persuaded that the main assault would be launched across the Straits of Dover against the Calais area, and, in fact, the Germans did so believe).

Among those present were a number of newspapermen in uniform, including Lieutenant Commander Barry Bingham, United States Naval Reserve, formerly of the *Louisville Courier-Journal.* One British representative, a Mr. C. P. Robertson, not otherwise identified in the minutes, said it would be a great help if SHAEF would indicate what it wanted to put across. "Do you want to put across that we are making great preparations?"[15]

After discussing various plans, the officers agreed on a formula governing coverage of various secret training and supply facilities. One naval officer warned that "It was not what the correspondent submitted for censorship but what he talked about in Fleet Street when he got back that mattered"—a realistic, cautionary note sounded by the military in later wars.

In the same meeting on April 24, 1944, General Davis expressed concern about the growing tendency among the military to impugn correspondents. "We take them in, make them subject to the Articles of War, put them in a uniform, and can execute them if necessary. Most of them are men of tremendous responsibility." Brigadier William Turner of the British Army said that an answer was needed to the question, "Is it SHAEF's policy that within the subsequently agreed security policy we are to go all out to arrange facilities [for the press] or to discourage them?" The answer was generally: Go all out.[16]

As early as March 1944, SHAEF planned the handling and transmission of press copy back from forward positions to home offices or London bureaus on D-Day. All of this was under military control. On the invasion beaches, for example, when a correspondent finished his story, he was to turn it over to his "conducting military public information officer." This public relations officer was to put it in a special press bag and hand it over to the dispatch point for cross-Channel boat delivery. If the bag contained several stories, before being dispatched the public relations officer should include, for the benefit of London censors, a priority sheet of stories based on the time each batch of copy was received and/or the type of story. If radio was operating from the beaches, the public relations officer was supposed to be responsible for handing copy to field press censors working with each wireless unit.[17]

How much advance notice were the correspondents to get? As laid out by General McClure on April 12, 1944, correspondents attached to SHAEF in London were not to be briefed in advance of D-Day. It was proposed that they be summoned for briefing not earlier than *one hour* prior to the time selected for publication of the initial communique—whose wording had already been decided several weeks in advance. Briefing was to be confined to the barest facts that the enemy might be expected to know. Suitable background information regarding the nature of amphibious operations and the technical problems involved would be given as thought advisable. No Allied order of battle or indication of unit strength would be given.[18]

The correspondents attached to assault forces would be briefed just prior to embarkation of elements of the first wave. This briefing would include only the fact that the operation was to be launched. Additional briefings at this time for the few correspondents actually accompanying the assault waves would include only sufficient orientation to enable them to cover their respective beaches. Timing of these briefings would be such that there would be no opportunity to compare notes with correspondents not leaving or with correspondents going to other beaches.[19]

And on April 12, General McClure wrote to Eisenhower's chief of staff, Lieutenant General Walter Bedell Smith, spelling out what would happen on D-Day in terms of press: "It is quite possible that the press of the United States and the United Kingdom will depend largely in the earliest period upon news emanating from communiques, material picked up on the South Coast [of England], material at press conferences, government statements, and enemy and neutral agency reports, broadcasts, and pictures." He added:

> The Allied publics are keyed up to expect a great volume of dramatic news as soon as the "second front" opens. If adequate news is not available from official Allied sources, the [home-front newspapers and radio] will certainly make immediate use of news from enemy and neutral sources together with comment and speculation based thereon. Neither censorship nor guidance, however high, can stop this.

McClure urged maximum use of high-level press conferences for "bridging this news gap," as well as briefings by key staff officers close to Eisenhower.[20]

Other planning documents dealt with accommodations, accreditation, pooling, and so forth. All accredited civilian correspondents would have the assimilated rank of captain in the U.S. Army or major in the British Army.[21] A complete London information service would be provided by SHAEF for all accredited war correspondents with a press information room and a reference library, staffed twenty-four hours a day. It made provision for briefing by all military components, with a briefing if possible once each twenty-four hours.[22]

The date on which war correspondents would be mobilized and instructed to join the forces by which they were to be accommodated would be given by SHAEF to its subordinate headquarters, which would then issue the necessary instructions for mobilizing correspondents.[23]

A total of 461 reporters and photographers from the Allied press and radio were accredited to SHAEF for D-Day, 180 of them Americans (perhaps half the number of American journalists who were to assemble in Barbados for the Grenada affair thirty-nine years later).[24]

On April 18, 1944, General Smith laid down the rules that were to govern censorship. He said:

> In general, the following information will not be released:
>
> (1) Reports likely to supply military information to the enemy to the detriment of the Allied war effort.
> (2) Unauthenticated, inaccurate or false reports, misleading statements and rumors.
> (3) Reports likely to injure the morale of the Allied Forces.[25]

Correspondents were told in great detail what would be regarded as censurable material:

> Notes for war correspondents accredited to SHAEF:
>
> The following is a selection of some of the more obvious things which the enemy intelligence always wants to know:
>
> (i) What our plans and intentions are.
> (ii) How strong our forces are, and of what formation and units they are composed.
> (iii) Where our forces are.
> (iv) What ports, bases and airfield we are using.
> (v) Where our supply dumps are, the extent of our supplies and what they comprise.
> (vi) Any new equipment or weapons we may have.
> (vii) Details of any new tactics we use, and of new tactical uses of existing weapons.
> (viii) What effect his attacks, gunfire, bombing have had on us and whether he has accomplished his purpose (e.g., hit the target in an air attack).

(ix) What our casualties are, either in number or by percentage.

(x) What the state of *our* intelligence information is.

(xi) Any information about our use of radar and radio.

(xii) Any information about our codes and cyphers.[26]

In April 1944, there were some disagreements which went as high as Eisenhower's chief of staff, General Smith, over the accreditation of various correspondents. On April 25, 1944, in a memorandum, General Davis, chief of the public relations division, wrote to Smith on "War correspondents concerning whom some question has arisen." In looking over the master list of correspondents, his superiors had expressed some doubts about accrediting them for D-Day, and General Davis defended them:

Wes Gallagher, Associated Press. Considered by Gen. McClure as a potential trouble-maker. Gallagher is considered by Associated Press to be its best war correspondent in this theater.

Frederick Kuh, *Chicago Sun.* Kuh is considered unreliable by Gen. McClure. Kuh is head of the *Chicago Sun*'s London Bureau and considered by that paper its best man in the theater.

Pierre Huss, INS [International News Service]. Considered by Gen. McClure to be untrustworthy. Considered by Lt. Gen. Smith to be at least lacking security-mindedness. Huss is head of the INS London Bureau.[27]

General Davis warned that lifting their credentials would cause an uproar among newsmen. No action was taken against them.[28]

On May 11, Eisenhower told newsmen:

At my first Press Conference as Supreme Commander I told the war correspondents that once they were accredited to my headquarters I considered them quasi-staff officers.

All war correspondents that may accompany the expedition are first accredited to Supreme Headquarters and operate under policies approved by the Supreme Commander. They are, in turn, assigned to lower headquarters in accordance with agreements between the Public Relations Division of this headquarters and the Public Relations Officers on the staffs of the several Commanders-in-Chief. This allocation is always limited by accommodations available. Public Relations Officers of the various echelons act as their guides. As a matter of policy accredited war correspondents should be accorded the greatest possible latitude in the gathering of legitimate news.

Consequently it is desired that, subject always to the requirements of operations, of which the Commander on the spot must be the sole judge, Commanders of all echelons and Public Relations Officers and Conducting Officers give accredited war correspondents all reasonable assistance. They should be allowed to talk freely with officers and enlisted personnel and to see the machinery of war in operation in order to visualize and transmit to the public the conditions under which the men from their countries are waging war against the enemy.[29]

The SHAEF staff also sent a memorandum to General Smith, who used it when he spoke to correspondents in late May. Prepared less than a month in advance of the landing in Normandy, it illustrates some of the traditional military views of correspondents (and of public affairs officers), views held even by those who understood the correspondents' duty in wartime:

General Eisenhower has said that I would tell you more about those things which you may expect to encounter in the field. There are many of you here who could describe the lot of the war correspondent under combat conditions better than I but I will give you some of the background from the commander's point of view.

There is no need to elaborate on the dangers that you are to face. The record of war correspondents in this war and the list of casualties speaks [sic] for itself. However, needless exposure to danger serves no one. A wounded or dead correspondent doesn't produce any copy except the story of his own misfortune—and that has to be written by someone else.

We recognize that there are two controlling forces in your work. First, to get the facts. Second, to get them to your medium of publication, press or radio. It is our job to see that you are provided with the proper opportunity to do both. This is easy to say but it is not as easy to do.

The great problems are transportation and communications. It would be ideal if we could provide each one of you with a personal driver, a jeep and a walkie-talkie tuned to London but that is out of the question. To spread you out, one each to a detachment of troops, would be easier for us and would give you more comfortable living. You would get the story but you wouldn't be able to get it back. You must be reasonably close to communications if you are working on spot news.

While on the subject of communications, we are to rely on air courier service and radio in the early days. Obviously this means that the air courier service must be located near an advanced airfield. Radio is a bit more flexible but, there too, it has its limitations. Initially, there will be movable radio sending sets but their wordage is limited. The fixed sets can clear much greater traffic. The result of this is that in many cases it will be of greater advantage for you to work in groups. This will give you not only better communications but will give you an opportunity to be briefed and get the overall picture. Naturally, in the early days the radio facilities will have to be rationed.

The transportation problem, aside from the limited number of vehicles available, also offers a problem to correspondents. The crowded conditions of roads eats [sic] into valuable time and sometimes nullifies the enterprise of a correspondent. Take the case of a group wishing to visit a certain division. The distance is not great but the roads are jammed with transport. There were cases in the Mediterranean theater where a single bridge formed a bottleneck which took eight hours to pass. Naturally, the car carrying the correspondents would have to wait its turn to get across. It will be a case of weighing the value of the story against the time consumed in getting it— that is for your judgment.

Another thing that comes to mind is the attitude of a commander engaged in combat. No commander wants a group of a dozen or more correspondents around his command post or observation post, not because he is unsociable or doesn't want to be helpful, but a group of that sort draws fire. The enemy is quick to take advantage of any unusual activity and has been known to use an 88mm anti-tank gun for sniping. A *pair* [emphasis added] of correspondents might be all right provided they are not interfering with operations. You will find that the great majority of commanders will not only cooperate but will welcome correspondents, for you bring to him contacts with the outside world and new points of view.

For those of you who will not go in the field but will be covering the overall developments as they are gathered at Headquarters I can assure you that every effort is being made to see that you will get the picture as rapidly as it is unfolded to us. The Public Relations Division of this headquarters aims to give you the very best in information and communication. I have its plans and, while I am not a newspaperman, I feel certain that you will be happy—that is as happy as a good correspondent will allow himself to be—with arrangements. I know and you know that no matter how much is given a newspaperman he wants more. Well, we will try to give you that "more." Please do not take this as an invitation for grousing in order to get extra facilities because we are keenly sensible of what you want and don't have to be clubbed into action. You have true friends at court in the Public Relations officers most of whom have had newspaper experience and have your slant uppermost in their minds. And, confidentially, sometimes we, in other branches at headquarters, wonder which they really are— newspapermen or officers. I don't think you have to worry on that score. If they can get it for you they will.[30]

The Association of American Correspondents on May 6 in London unanimously passed a resolution thanking Brigadier General Davis of Eisenhower's headquarters for the arrangements to facilitate press coverage of the invasion of Western Europe. The resolution was proposed by Raymond Daniell of *The New York Times* and seconded by Virgil Pinkley, general European manager of United Press.[31]

As *The New York Times* reported from London on May 26, 1944:

All the blueprints for second front news coverage look beautiful on paper but many newspapermen are keeping their fingers crossed because they have not forgotten the many snags that interfered with the transmission of news when Allied forces landed in North Africa [in 1942]. Those dispatches either never reached the home office, or got there in fragments several days apart.[32]

The article went on to note that, during the upcoming invasion, there would be two communiques issued, one at 11:00 A.M. British time, and the other at 11:30 P.M. British time:

American correspondents are particularly unhappy. Like newspapermen anywhere they feel that they represent the reading public. They point out that a communique issued at 11 A.M. in London (which is six hours ahead of New York in summer and five hours ahead the rest of the year) will just miss the morning editions in New York unless their papers go to extra expense of holding open far beyond their regular closing time.[33]

*   *   *

The assignment list for D-Day was made out well in advance. Every correspondent accredited to SHAEF was assigned to either Supreme Headquarters or to various echelons of the land, naval, and air contingents. For example, Walter Cronkite, then of the United Press, was assigned to Supreme Headquarters Air, as were eight other U.S. newsmen. Scripps-Howard's famed columnist Ernie Pyle and *The New Yorker*'s A. J. Liebling (whose name was misspelled "Leveling") were also on the list. British newsmen outnumbered American newsmen overall by 188 to 180, not counting another twenty-seven from the British Empire.[34] The press also had reporters based back at Supreme Headquarters in London to receive and expand on the communiques; for example, CBS assigned Edward R. Murrow to this role.[35]

Relatively few reporters were allowed to go in on the assault phase. For example, with the entire U.S. First Army, landing at Omaha and Utah beaches, there were assigned a total of twenty U.S. correspondents and photographers and newsreel people. And not all of these were landing in the first wave. Of the twenty men, seven were with the three American wire services; three were with U.S. newspapers, and one each came from the three major networks serving radio.[36] Four were photographers in a picture pool. The remaining three represented *The New Yorker, Stars & Stripes,* and the newsreel pool. In addition, because the overall landing force, which consisted of British and Canadian as well as American forces, was so dispersed and so large, each group of journalists tended to cover the troops of their respective countries.

Out of the total number (180) of American correspondents accredited to SHAEF there were only twenty-seven U.S. newsmen for radio, films, and print going ashore with elements of all three armies: the British Second Army, the Canadian First Army, and the U.S. First Army. Other journalists destined to follow the initial assault were to come in later, and the rest would remain in London.

Inevitably, some discussion occurred among the military concerning the call-up for duty of correspondents who were going to go cross-Channel with their units. The big question was when the correspondents would be summoned to report to the units that they would accompany on D-Day. The British, who were uneasy about this, had repeatedly raised the problem of security; in fact, on January 28, 1944, Winston Churchill had written to General Eisenhower suggesting that a "very stringent attitude should be adopted in regard to communication to the press correspondents in this country of any background information about Overlord operations either before they start or while they proceed."[37] Even so, reporters had been summoned quietly and gone on training exercises with Allied troops long before D-Day.

On June 2, Lieutenant General Smith, Eisenhower's chief of staff, told the worried British War Cabinet that correspondents would be called up for duty at times varying between D-Day minus six and D-Day minus two.[38] He outlined the security precautions imposed on all war correspondents and concluded:

> It is not felt that a particularly dangerous "flag" will be hoisted in Fleet Street when these correspondents are alerted. For only 40 [British and American] correspondents are taking part in the initial phase and these 40 will not depart in a body. Further, as many as 25 correspondents have attended [training] exercises in the past and no great comment was caused by their disappearance.[39]

As near as can be ascertained, the American correspondents did not accompany every element of the invasion force. Only six were on Omaha Beach, which turned out to be a pivotal battle, involving two U.S. divisions. No American correspondent accompanied the Ranger forces near Omaha Beach. Only one, *Time*'s William Walton, accompanied the U.S. airborne units, whose men parachuted behind the enemy beach defenses in Normandy. The British allowed Leonard Mosley of the Kemsley newspapers to drop in with the British airborne troops. He filed a dispatch on June 6 that was delayed for forty-eight hours but saw wide distribution.[40]

How did things work out in practice? The news of the invasion came out of London. On June 10, 1944, *The New York Times* reported that the army's communications system set up for correspondents accompanying American troops on the assault on France broke down completely. For more than twenty-eight hours they were unable to get news out on the troops in action.[41] (The British did not have the same problem.)

On June 10 the Associated Press reported from London that some 2.5 million words telling the story of the invasion had been sent by more than 300 Allied war correspondents through London cable facilities to the United States and the British Empire. The flow of words increased from 400,000 filed on June 6 to 800,000 on June 9; 100 pictures were also being filed daily.[42]

But let John MacVane of NBC tell the story of the assault phase on Omaha Beach:

I . . . was driven to a correspondents' training camp near Bristol, where the public relations officers and the new correspondents had been learning what to do in the field. Some other reporters were already there, and we were put into tents under the wet pine trees. At the mess hall that night, rain swirled and drummed hideously on the roof. Some of the correspondents in the mess were new to me. Times had changed since the early days of the war when we all knew one another. So many correspondents had arrived from America and so many new ones had been assigned to war reporting by the British papers that we had never even seen the faces of several.

After dinner we were told to draw special equipment. Each of us received five boxes of K rations, concentrated food in waterproof boxes. We were given waterproofed matchboxes, pills to purify drinking water, extra cigarettes, pills for seasickness, and even the means to make love safe and sanitary, which were also useful for waterproofing small articles in our pockets.

We were about twenty-five or thirty in all, but not all of us were going with the assault troops. [Columnist] Ernie Pyle, for instance, was to be with Bradley at First Army Headquarters, which would probably not reach France for a couple of days after the invasion. Others would be with naval command ships and might never get on shore at all. . . .

There were only three of us . . . with our old friends of the 1st division. . . .[43]

We three correspondents went to . . . the Coast Guard ship *Samuel Chase*. An alternative headquarters had been set up on this ship so that if the *Ancon* were sunk, Gen. Wyman could immediately take over the direction of the battle. With him he had the assistant chief of each section. Also on board was the headquarters of the primary assault regiment, the 16th Infantry, and full battalion of that regiment.

When we were aboard, Major Gale said to us, "We don't think you three reporters should go ashore together. If your boat were sunk, and it may well be sunk, the division would lose all its reporters together."[44]

[The reporters landed on Omaha Beach amid chaos.]

It stays light very late in Normandy during June. It must have been six or seven o'clock when Gen. Huebner, the division commander, arrived, and after a time he moved the division command post a mile or so inland. Our advance troops were fighting a short distance farther in, as well as on our flanks at the villages of St. Laurent and Colleville. The Lee Moulins exit had not yet been taken, and the 116th Regiment of the 29th Division had a hard baptism of fire.

. . . At times a machine gun would start clattering in the woods, and one would see leaves and branches clipped above one's head. As soon as a few shots had been fired in any particular place, signs would be posted, Sniper Up This Road. Dead Germans at various points showed where the fighting had been fiercest. Sometimes the bodies of Americans would be lying nearby. When a machine gun started firing, the nearest American unit would start looking for it, so that there were little battles all around us. There was no real front at this time, only groups of American troops in various places fighting little battles and then trying to move on.

Lieut. Sam Brightman [later a Democratic National Committee spokesman] showed up in the late afternoon. He was the only Army public relations officer on Omaha that day. All the vast public relations preparations, and only Brightman, a lieutenant, there to help us. He had no means of communication, but when we all wrote short dispatches, he volunteered to take them to the beach and give them to some Navy officer in the hope of passing them along by hand to England. We entrusted our messages to Sam, but none of them ever arrived in London. I thought I had arranged things well for my broadcasting from the beach, but Lieutenant Colonel Pickett, the division signal officer, told me that all four of the radios he expected to have had been sunk before they reached shore. . . .[45]

Censorship did not cause undue delay, once the stories got to London. *The New York Times* reported on June 13 from London in a story by E. C. Daniel that it took only an average of eleven minutes apiece for invasion news dispatches to be read and censored by the three-nation military censorship team at SHAEF.[46]

Almost inevitably the newsmen in Normandy formed a beachhead correspondents' committee, headed by John Thompson of the *Chicago Tribune*,[47] to deal with problems of the press. They were primarily problems of transport and communications.

Later, in July 1944, reassuring the British, Colonel R. Ernest Depuy, acting chief of the public relations division, wrote to Major General C.M.F. White of the Twenty-first Army Group, soothing his anger over reporters' complaints over communications. Illustrating the SHAEF attitude, Depuy said:

I do not know whether you have any specific case in mind, and none has been reported in connection with the present operations, but our experience is that, if the correspondents are taken into our confidence and understand the security background, so that they can write good stories without coming into conflict with censorship, there is very little trouble with them. If, however, they feel that they are being hampered in reporting events, they are apt to react, not altogether unnaturally, by trying to beat the censor.

I am sure all your officers are anxious to assist the correspondents, and that if we can work together to this end, many of the difficulties can easily be overcome. I feel that the basic approach of the staff to this matter should be one not of suspicion and prejudice, but *one of confidence in and acceptance of the correspondents as an integral part of the whole set-up.*[48]

Depuy's letter followed a bit of a flap among British newspapermen in Normandy who complained that the Americans, after losing out initially, were getting better communications and facilities than their British counterparts. One of the complainers was Alan Moorehead, who left the British sector to join the U.S. forces and report the fall of the port of Cherbourg.

He was quoted as saying, not without envy:

Correspondents attached to the American Army are treated as active officers and given the equipment to do their job. They are entrusted with vehicles and drivers. Each division has a Press officer, who provides a courier service to get correspondents' messages back to a radio station. Generals constantly invite correspondents to spend a day touring the front with them. . . .

British correspondents there, with their own armies, are regarded with a good deal of suspicion; not by the fighting men, but by the organisation [Twenty-first Army Group] that controls them.

An officer must accompany each one of us where ever we go. Technically, if I want a haircut an officer must come and watch me get it. I may not drive an Army vehicle.

We have a radio set that sends some 80 words a minute—when it works. Further, we are limited to a maximum of 400 words, whereas the Americans have no limit for their 700-word-a-minute transmitter.

Moorehead had been told that there is no prospect of correspondents receiving additional facilities. His first two dispatches took eight days to reach England; his third was lost altogether.[49]

Whatever the flaws of D-Day arrangements and the later problems of coverage, they represented a major advance over journalists' earlier travails. Joe Alex Morris, foreign editor of the United Press, described his experience in preparing for two Allied attacks in 1942, the August raid on Dieppe and the November invasion of North Africa:

The [disastrous] Dieppe raid [by 6,000 British and Canadian troops] was an example of how not to do it. Only broadline arrangements were made in advance, upon the insistence of correspondents, for newspapermen [based in London] to accompany Commando troops occasionally on raids against the European coast. The American Correspondents' Association submitted to the British War Office a list of names drawn by lot and the War Office theoretically selected the men in rotation.

Under this system, men were summoned secretly for a period of training with the Commando troops and assigned to an operation. They might be out of touch with their offices for two or three weeks, after which they would go on a raid or, if the operation was called off for some reason, return to London. Some of these reporters also went on raids about which they have never been permitted to write.

No information was given newspapermen in advance regarding the Dieppe raid, but a limited number of correspondents were told to report secretly for assignment. Combined Operations Headquarters then told the censorship that nothing was to be passed regarding what happened at Dieppe unless it was written by the reporters who accompanied the troops and that their stories were to be pooled and made available to everyone after they returned to London.[50]

This resulted in two days of endless confusion in which a great part of the real story of the operation was held up until the censorship eventually was forced to change its instructions. The secrecy which the [British] Combined Operations Command considered essential also resulted in some wild [wire service] reports [in America] that the raid was a "second front" invasion.

The handling of the North African operation showed considerable improvement. Weeks before the invasion date [November 8, 1942], the executive committee of the American Correspondents' Association [in London] met with a United States general in charge of press relations. . . .

Reporters later were selected from the lists we had submitted and were told to report quietly by twos or threes, prepared for a journey of indefinite length. The North African invasion was such a big operation that an unexpectedly large number of correspondents vanished from London during a single week, a total of five being taken from the United Press bureau alone. . . .[51]

As far as can be ascertained, the London censorship of press dispatches prior to the Normandy invasion was largely effective. We do not know what rumors or reports reached Germany from its agents, if any, mingling with newsmen in the bars and restaurants on Fleet Street. The chief breach of security prior to June 6, 1944 that is on record came from an *official* handout put out by the Allied air forces and was noticed by none other than Winston Churchill. The offending material had been passed by the Americans; it was a headline on an official picture of Ninth Air Force bombing activity which said, " 'Softening Up' the Invasion Coast" (published in *The New York Times* on May 28). The caption under the picture was "A-20 Havocs of the 9th Air Force blasting Nazi road junction in northern France."[52] A sharp rebuke went to the Ninth Air Force Public Relations Office on May 27 for allowing this pinpointing detail to get through in an official handout.[53] The Germans apparently did not notice.

On the other hand, the little-opposed invasion of southern France in August 1944 was, as the Associated Press reported on August 15, the worst-kept secret of the war:

> Thousands of Frenchmen and Americans knew it was coming. Correspondents in Normandy and Brittany were constantly asked about it by both Frenchmen and soldiers. The question was among the first asked by Frenchmen in captured towns. Probably the French underground was told of the impending invasion and they told everyone else.[54]

There were also plenty of press complaints about military secrecy during the war in the European theater. Blackouts of political news out of Algiers after the assassination of Admiral Jean Darlan in 1942 provoked an outcry among reporters in Algiers. There was a furor on both sides of the Atlantic regarding news from the hard-pressed Anzio beachhead in February 1944, following orders for a blackout issued by a British general, Sir Harold R.L.G. Alexander, commander of Allied forces. Critics in Parliament alleged that Alexander was trying to impose censorship for policy as well as security reasons.[55]

Alexander had required that news dispatches be sent by courier to Naples for censorship rather than being transmitted from the beachhead by available radio. But the secretary of war, Henry L. Stimson, told a press conference in Washington "that my only comment on that is that in accord with my usual policy, General Henry Maitland Wilson commanding in the Mediterranean theater is in the best possible position to judge whether factors such as you refer to affect operations in this theater either favorably or adversely."[56]

According to *The New York Times,* Norman Clark, representing the combined British press on the hard-pressed beachhead, said that restrictions were due to official displeasure at Allied headquarters over some dispatches that had "compared the beachhead at Anzio to Dunkirk."[57]

There were also major mishaps that occurred during the war that were blacked out by censorship, notably the shooting down by American anti-aircraft fire of American transport planes carrying paratroopers during the Sicily invasion in July 1943.[58]

*   *   *

In Italy in 1944, CBS's Eric Sevareid accompanied U.S. troops; and years later, he reflected on what he saw. Ground combat, as television reporters were to discover in Vietnam, does not really make for comprehensive "visuals":

> One never saw masses of men assaulting the enemy. What one observed, in apparently unrelated patches, was small, loose bodies of men moving down narrow defiles or over steep inclines, going methodically from position to position between long halts, and the only continuous fact was the roaring and crackling of the big guns.
>
> One felt baffled at first by the unreality of it all. Unseen groups of men were fighting other men that they rarely saw. They located the enemy by the abstractions of mathematics, an imagined science; they reported the enemy through radio waves that no man could visualize; and they destroyed him most frequently with projectiles no eye could follow. When the target became quiet, that particular fight would be over and they moved ahead to something else. Never were there masses of men in olive drab locked in photogenic combat with masses of men in field gray. It was slow, spasmodic movement from one patch of silence to another. . . .

At one point, Sevareid found himself with some GIs in a newly captured town:

> A young German soldier lay sprawled just inside a sagging doorway, his hobnailed boots sticking into the street. Two American soldiers were resting and smoking cigarettes a few feet away, paying the body no attention. "Oh, him?" one of them said in response to a question. "Son of a bitch kept lagging behind the others when we brought them in. We got tired of hurrying him up all the time." Thus casually was deliberate murder announced by boys who a year before had taken no lives but those of squirrel or pheasant. I found that I was not shocked nor indignant; I was merely a little surprised. As weeks went by and this experience was repeated many times, I ceased even to be surprised—only, I could never again bring myself to write or speak with indignation of the Germans' violations of the "rules of warfare."[59]

Unlike some of his later colleagues in CBS, Sevareid had no illusions about the truth of battle as conveyed by journalism or about the difference between the experiences of war correspondents and of soldiers:

> . . . only the soldier really lives the war. The journalist does not. He may [occasionally] share the soldier's outward life and dangers, but he cannot share his inner life because the same moral compulsion does not bear upon him. The [journalist] observer knows he has alternatives of action; the soldier knows he has none. It is the mere knowing which makes the difference. Their worlds are very far apart, for one is free, the other a slave.

This war must be seen to be believed, but it must be lived to be understood. We [journalists] can tell you only of the events, of what men do. We cannot really tell you how or why they do it. We can see, and tell you, that this war is brutalizing some among your sons and yet ennobling others. We can tell you very little more. . . .

If, by the miracles of art and genius, in later years two or three among [the veterans] can open their hearts and the right words come, then perhaps we shall all know a little of what [World War II] was like. And we shall know, then, that all the present speakers and writers hardly touched the story.[60]

· 3 ·

THE KOREAN WAR:
LAISSEZ-FAIRE TO CENSORSHIP

T
HE 1950-53 Korean War, as anyone over fifty may recall, rapidly became an extremely unpopular conflict among Americans at
home. "Korea, Communism, and Corruption" became a
Republican slogan against the Truman administration in 1952, and the
costs and frustrations of this "limited war" against Communist aggression helped to put Dwight D. Eisenhower in the White House.

This frustration was largely exploited by the Right, not by the Left
as happened later when the United States fought in Vietnam, and involved neither the professoriat nor the students. The protest was sub-
sumed in regular party politics, but neither Republicans nor Democrats
came to advocate U.S. withdrawal from Korea. As it turned out, the war
lasted only three years (albeit with U.S. losses of 34,000 dead), and
its progress could be measured conventionally in terms of ground gained
or lost, even after it settled into a military stalemate in late 1951. The
attendant destruction of Korean cities and towns and heavy civilian loss
of life produced few outcries at home. War was war.

In terms of military-media relations, the Korean War commenced with
a U.S. experiment with "voluntary censorship." This proved unworkable
and was followed by a return, at the request of many newsmen, to formal military censorship on the World War II model. Television cameras
made their first battlefield appearance but played a minor role in the
news flow. In contrast to 1941-45, some newsmen violated the rules
(none was punished); some fraternized (after July 1951) with the foe
during the truce talks at Panmunjom; and in general, the press, like the
politicians back home, was more critical. This period was also the beginning of the changes in communications—notably the use of long-distance
telephones—that were later to affect both war coverage and military
security. But, on the whole, the relationship worked.

The war began as a surprise.

On Saturday, June 24, 1950, almost five years after the end of World War II, while President Harry S. Truman was attending a family reunion in Independence, Missouri, he was informed that the North Koreans had crossed the Thirty-eighth Parallel and were threatening the South Korean capital of Seoul.

It was not clear at first whether it was the latest of a series of border raids against the poorly equipped, undermanned South Korean Army or an invasion. Truman did not immediately return to Washington. Instead he told Secretary of State Dean Acheson to alert the United Nations. The United Nations, then located at Lake Success on Long Island, New York, had been trying for several years to arrange elections for a unified Korean government and claimed legal authority over all of that country.

At the Security Council meeting the next day, Secretary General Trygve Lie (of Norway) called for a resolution, which was subsequently adopted, demanding an immediate cease-fire and withdrawal by the North Koreans. Two days later a second resolution was adopted urging full-scale United Nations military support for South Korea, which by then was clearly the victim of an all-out invasion. These resolutions were adopted in the absence of the Soviet delegate, Jacob Malik, who had been boycotting the Security Council for five months in protest against its refusal to give the seat of Nationalist China to the People's Republic of China.

Meanwhile, after two days of secret intensive discussions with his cabinet, President Truman announced that the United States would defend South Korea under the auspices of the United Nations. Even as he spoke, he had already committed U.S. air and naval power. Although it was to shift six months later, public opinion largely supported the stand taken by Truman, and that support was bipartisan. The man he had bested in the 1948 presidential election, Thomas Dewey, sent a wire saying, "I wholeheartedly agree with and support the difficult decision you have made," and even the conservative Senator Robert Taft of Ohio said the country should go "all-out."

Strong support came from Western Europe, where it was felt that Truman had saved the United Nations and relieved a little of the Soviet pressure on Europe. President Truman's decision was influenced by the perceived danger to American security interests in Asia, particularly in Japan, and by the large body of postwar expert opinion, which held that World War II could have been forestalled had a firm stand been taken early against Nazi aggression. The Truman decision also followed five years of increasing tension vis-a-vis the Soviet Union and Eastern Europe—notably the Berlin Blockade of 1948-49, the Communist takeover of Czechoslovakia in 1948, and the Greek Civil War pitting the government against Communist guerrillas, a war that lasted through the late 1940s and ended only after Tito's Yugoslavia cut off support to the Greek Communists by closing the border with Greece.[1] But Truman did not ask Congress for a declaration of war, even as he mobilized the reserves, curtailed federal domestic programs, and later imposed certain wartime economic controls—steps not taken in 1965, when the Johnson administration committed troops to Vietnam.

On June 30, 1950, Truman received a cable from General Douglas MacArthur, American commander in Japan, saying, "The South Korean forces are in confusion, have not seriously fought, and lack leadership. . . . It is essential that the enemy advance be held or its impetus will threaten the over-running of all Korea."[2] The immediate commitment of U.S. forces was the only way to retrieve the situation, MacArthur said. Truman authorized MacArthur to send a battalion combat team to the battle zone and, later that day, permitted MacArthur to commit all of his forces, ordering a naval blockade of North Korea.

And so, less than five years after the defeat of Japan, Americans were again involved in a serious shooting war. But this time, after an initial period of popularity, intense opposition arose on the home front, particularly after the Chinese Communist forces entered the war.

In terms of the American press, only the wire services had correspondents on duty in Seoul (which fell to the North Koreans on June 27, 1950). The available U.S. correspondents were in Tokyo, capital of American-occupied Japan and headquarters of General MacArthur, who was both supreme Allied commander and head of the U.S. Far East Command (FEC). (Until war broke out, his responsibilities did not include Korea.) Under UN auspices, he was also to become supreme commander of the UN forces.

The initial press reports of the North Korean invasion came from the wire services (Associated Press, United Press, and International News Service) out of Seoul and out of Tokyo. During the first days of July, as poorly-armed U.S. troops from the army's understrength Twenty-fourth Infantry Division on garrison duty in Japan moved by sea and air to Pusan and then up to Taegu and later to Taejon to bolster the reeling South Korean units, American newsmen went with them. It was a time of desperation for American troops, and it was an extremely difficult story for the press—not only difficult but dangerous.

As John Hohenberg notes:

Peter Kalischer of the UP watched the first American infantrymen go into action in Korea on July 5, watched them break and run before Communist tanks, and himself narrowly escaped capture. When he walked into a makeshift pressroom at Taejon nearly three days later, he had a tragic story to tell. But neither he nor any of the other seventy correspondents who had come to Korea by that time (only five had been around at the beginning) could get much out unless they flew back to Japan.

In 24th Division headquarters at Taejon, there was only one military line to Tokyo over which the correspondents could telephone messages. They had to stand in line, rationed to a few minutes each, and dictate bulletins or detail. The bad news came in small doses.[3]

For the military, providing news representatives with logistical support became a sizable command responsibility. By September 1, 238 reporters, both American and foreign, were accredited in Tokyo to cover operations in Korea (eventually there were 270). The best estimates were that fewer than a quarter of those accredited were ever at the front at one time. As for the hard day-to-day coverage, according to Hohenberg, relatively few stuck it out, but among them were veterans of World War II. (All told, ten American correspondents died during the fighting, mostly during the first few months. One photographer, Frank Noel of AP, was captured by Chinese Communists on December 1, 1950; he spent over two and a half years in Communist prison camps.)[4]

In July 1950, with no fewer than seventy correspondents on hand, the U.S. Eighth Army commander, Lieutenant General Walton H. Walker, had an extra burden to carry when he set up his command post at Taegu. Besides such personal needs as post-exchange cards, authorization to buy field clothing, clearance to enter the combat zone, travel orders, billeting, and mess facilities, accredited correspondents received from the FEC or the Eighth Army their prime requirements: transportation and communication facilities. In Taegu, the Eighth Army information officer established a correspondents' billet in a schoolhouse.

Oddly enough, General MacArthur, although authorized by Washington to impose censorship, refused to do so, declaring it "abhorrent," in July 1950. Instead he tossed the problem to the newsmen. Write what you please, he said, in effect, but if you break security or make "unwarranted criticisms," you will be held responsible personally.[5]

This permissive policy pleased no one. Howard Handleman, then Tokyo bureau chief for INS, said recently that "in early July, a bunch of us [bureau chiefs] sneaked into MacArthur's headquarters and asked him to impose censorship." Without it, the competitive pressures to disclose more information than the rival reporter were enormous. "What might endanger the troops was a matter of judgment," Handleman said. The wire-service reporter who was least sensitive to security matters "got the play" in newspapers at home. "Every one of us did it."[6] The group included Walt Simmons of the *Chicago Tribune*, Lindesay Parrott of *The New York Times*, AP's Russ Brines, and Earnest Hoberecht of the UP.

One experienced reporter, Tom Lambert of the AP, was briefly barred from the battlefront in mid-July—although he, too, had asked for censorship. (The ban on Lambert was lifted quickly by MacArthur.) What stirred MacArthur's subordinates was a line in Lambert's July 12 story that was denounced on other than "security" grounds. Reported *The New York Times* from Tokyo:

> The officer cited as an "aid and comfort to the enemy" an excerpt from one of Mr. Lambert's dispatches that quoted a front-line soldier saying, ". . . this is a damned useless war." The soldier's remark, which Colonel Echols quoted in part, was taken from a paragraph in Mr. Lambert's July 12 story, in which the soldier was quoted as follows: "You don't fight two tank-equipped divisions with .30 caliber carbines. I never saw such a useless damned war in all my life."
>
> Then Mr. Lambert went on to say that "bitter though they were, this G.I. band had fought a gallant delaying action against tremendous odds. . . ."[7]

In the absence of official censorship, said *The New York Times,* all reporters "have been left on their own to follow the Army's instructions that they write their stories with due regard for security factors." The correspondents found that the definition of security was so loose, even among army officers, that the correspondents could not adequately judge for themselves.[8]

The problem fell into two broad categories:

> One category is military security. No reporter has consciously violated known security rules. However, there have been serious leaks—most of them originating in the United States—concerning such matters as troop departures. Some [wire service] reporters have withheld news developments on the grounds of security only to learn that the story was used by a competitor. In some cases the information was not considered of security value by officers in a position to know, but there is considerable disagreement among the officers themselves. . . . The other category is military prestige. In the present retreating and holding warfare a lot of battle-green American youngsters are taking heavy punishment from experienced troops heavily outnumbering them. Their disillusionment has been reported in detail. Some officers believe this is bad for Army morale, bad for American public opinion and helpful to the enemy's morale. Whether any of these points are correct, there is a perceptible increase in sensitivity to these stories. Thus far, Tokyo correspondents have failed in repeated efforts to obtain regular briefings on the military situation. In the Korean war zone, field headquarters sends a spokesman twice a day to brief the press.[9]

But MacArthur's aides, despite public laments about security leaks and inquiries from the Pentagon, did not impose censorship. The general was convinced that it was unworkable. According to Colonel Melvin Voorhees, an Eighth Army censor:

Newsmen used their own discretion in reporting operations in Korea until late December 1950. During that time, the disclosure of security information by correspondents was virtually a daily occurrence. Contrary to the guidelines given them, newsmen prematurely revealed the withdrawal of United Nations troops to the Naktong River line, the arrival of the 2nd Infantry Division at Pusan, the amphibious landing of the 1st Cavalry Division at Pohangdung, the arrival in Korea of the first British troops, the 1st Marine Division's amphibious landing at Inchon (10 hours before it actually happened). . . . There were hundreds of other similar disclosures.[10]

The first breaches of security occurred within days of General MacArthur's request for voluntary censorship. MacArthur's admonition to newsmen changed nothing. Alarmed by the reports coming out of Korea, members of Congress, too, called on the press and radio to stop disclosing troop movements in the Far East. But security breaches continued.[11]

Perhaps remembering his coterie of journalists during World War II, General MacArthur was hospitable to newsmen before and during the landing of the First Marine Division (and follow-up Seventh Army Division troops) at Inchon on September 15, 1950. The landing had long been rumored. Keyes Beech later recalled that several dozen reporters were assembled in the Tokyo Press Club for assignments to various ships in the invasion fleet, then went off to join them in Sasebo and other ports of embarkation.[12]

Howard Handleman, the INS bureau chief, was taken with MacArthur and his staff to the command ship *Mount McKinley* along with the bureau chiefs of the AP and UP, and *Life* photographer Carl Mydans. They had good communications.[13]

However, the lack of common ground rules was highlighted once again. As *Newsweek* reported:

Attending a native-language press conference in Pusan, Bill Shinn, a Korean citizen and reporter for the Associated Press, heard about the invasion [from a South Korean general] three hours before Tokyo released the news. An hour after he rushed his story to a transmission station, military headquarters in Tokyo asked all wire services to kill any stories they might get on an invasion. It was too late. Some morning papers in America carried Shinn's accurate report and then Tokyo ordered all invasion stories released. Shinn, in the meantime, was reminded summarily by the Army that he had not been fully accredited as a correspondent. Temporarily he was denied use of Signal Corps phones from Korea to the AP in Tokyo. His stories, however, could still be filed by other AP men.[14]

As Keyes Beech recalled later, he got ashore aboard a landing craft with columnist Joseph Alsop in the seventh or eighth wave, saw a slice of what was going on, and got a ride out to MacArthur's command ship, which was the only place from which he or other reporters could transmit their stories. He sent a "color" story. So did the *New York Herald Tribune*'s Marguerite Higgins, who had gone ashore earlier. According to Beech and Handleman, several big-name newsmen (including Don Whitehead of AP and Homer Bigart of the *Herald Tribune)* were marooned on board a transport carrying follow-up Army Seventh Division troops. Their commander, presumably worried that his unit would lose out to the marines in terms of press coverage, refused to help the newsmen get ashore; they spent a day or two raging before they got free.[15]

No firm estimate of how or when many reporters and photographers went ashore at Inchon (Operation Chromite) seems available. But veterans seem to think at least thirty reporters were on hand. (Others were, of course, covering the U.S. breakout from the Pusan perimeter.) The problems of newsmen at Inchon, as in most Korean battles, did not spring from deliberate military policy, but from the communications difficulties and general confusion inherent in rapidly moving major operations. Not surprisingly, most of the overall detail on the initial D-Day landing came out of MacArthur's command ship or from Tokyo—again without censorship.

Although press revelations endangered lives, plans, and operations, no serious losses could be directly attributed to them. The changing tide of battle probably had an influence. By mid-September 1950, Allied forces, under the UN flag, were able to launch an offensive and in October moved deep into North Korea. The disorganized North Korean Army apparently was unable to take advantage of the information revealed by the American press. But the situation changed in November: numerically superior forces from Communist China entered Korea and began driving Allied forces southward. The foe thus regained the initiative and could exploit whatever information he could obtain. The Allies' need to conceal the identity, strength, and movement of friendly troops therefore assumed even greater importance.[16]

It was not until December 20, 1950, that the Far East Command imposed military censorship, after consulting news agency heads in Tokyo. "Effective immediately," the FEC information officer announced, "all press stories, radio broadcasts, magazine articles and photography pertaining to military operations" were to be submitted for clearance before transmission. Within the FEC public information office, a Press Advisory Division was established in Tokyo to handle the job of censoring the reports. In Korea, the Eighth Army organized a Press Security Division within its information office to perform censorship duties there.[17]

As one historian later noted:

> Some newsmen protested the invocation of military censorship. Complainants charged that the new rules of censorship were the most drastic in military

history. (Eighth Army censors initially employed a copy of World War II censorship rules.) Others complained that they were threatened with imprisonment. These, apparently, were referring to the fact that officially accredited U.S. press correspondents in war zones are subject, by Act of Congress, to the Uniform Code of Military Justice. With respect to security regulations, an Army legal opinion held that correspondents who failed to obey orders of the command with which they worked could be charged and tried under UCMJ Article 92. (There is no evidence that this opinion was ever tested before military or civil courts.) A few reporters claimed that censorship meant that all adverse criticism of military operations was to be suppressed. Apparently the military rule spurring this charge was that truth, *per se,* did not justify passing a fact through censorship, that even truth had to be suppressed if its disclosure would benefit the enemy.[18]

Most correspondents (90 percent of them, according to one estimate) favored World War II-style military censorship; they were convinced that no other process could ensure military security. Some reporters in Korea, as in Tokyo, actively sought military censorship as a means of reducing the harmful side effects of the keen competition among themselves.[19]

The imposition of military censorship, however, was no panacea. Though censors at FEC in Tokyo and Eighth Army Headquarters in Korea asked the same basic questions of material submitted to them, enough difference existed in the application of detailed criteria at each headquarters to create a variable kind of censorship.[20]

On the other hand, some newsmen found that the differences in judgment provided an advantageous system of appeals. If, for example, their material failed to clear Eighth Army censorship, they could submit it again, sometimes with success, to the Tokyo censor's office. Some security information thus reached the press.[21]

Nor was military censorship an insurmountable obstacle for those newsmen who chose to evade it. Under the established system in Korea, a correspondent was free, once his story was cleared by an Eighth Army censor, to phone his report to his Tokyo bureau or cable it to his home office. As predicted by the Eighth Army Public Information Officer in December 1950, this loophole was exploited by a few correspondents. For example, a prearranged code, called "twenty questions," was employed by some correspondents and their agency representatives in Tokyo to expand a cleared report. After a newsman had finished dictating his story from Korea to Tokyo over the phone, his Tokyo colleague would question him and receive answers as in the following:

Question: Are you coming over soon?
Translation: Do you expect that we will surrender Seoul?

Answer: I think so.
Translation: Yes.
Question: When do you expect to come?
Translation: When do you think we'll retreat from Seoul and go south of the Han River?
Answer: I'll try to leave in three or four days.
Translation: In the next three or four days.

"Twenty questions" lasted for only a short time. It was stopped when Eighth Army censors threatened to have correspondents guilty of such subterfuge expelled from Korea.[22]

But the subterfuge continued to be used when correspondents decided to ignore completely both censorship requirements and the express requests of the army commander. On January 3, 1951, as Eighth Army troops withdrew before numerically superior Chinese forces, the order was given to evacuate Seoul and drop behind the Han River just below the city. The critical withdrawal across the river of large numbers of UN troops and huge amounts of equipment could not be completed before the evening of January 4.

General Matthew B. Ridgway, who had taken command of the Eighth Army (after the death of Lieutenant General Walton Walker), therefore requested that correspondents help conceal the withdrawal from the enemy by holding their news stories of the event until the tactical move was completed. But by early morning of the 4th, the story already had appeared in print in the United States.

Three United Press men, two correspondents in Korea and the bureau manager in Japan, were responsible. Each had had access to army censors, but each had deliberately avoided them. The Eighth Army public information officer recommended to MacArthur's staff in Tokyo that the two correspondents in Korea be expelled and that the bureau manager in Tokyo be reported to his home office for disciplinary action. But MacArthur's headquarters took no action; the United Press ignored the incident. The editor-in-chief of International News Service, on the other hand, seemed to have been prompted by this incident to wire his Tokyo bureau manager that all INS members were to abide strictly by regulations and make no attempt to break censorship. "We place security far above any competitive advantage in reporting news," he stated.[23]

Censorship in the war zone also had its geographical limitations. Following the costly UN retreat from North Korea, a number of correspondents returned to the United States, where they went on lecture tours, prepared dramatic magazine articles, and received a variety of awards for distinguished reporting. As the military saw it, these often were achieved at the expense of misleading the American public.

As the Chinese Communists pushed south, in January 1951, for example, predictions of impending disaster by journalists were widely disseminated. Don Whitehead and Hal Boyle of the Associated Press saw the demise of the U.S. Eighth Army, and during the same month, Jim Lucas of Scripps-Howard stated that the Eighth Army would be out of Korea in six weeks. The censors in Korea and Japan, of course, could do nothing to curb "news analysis."

> In an effort to improve military censorship to the benefit of both newsmen and the command, GHQ, FEC, on 11 January 1951, redistributed censorship and press release responsibilities. From that date, the Eighth Army issued all information of ground operations and censored all copy submitted by correspondents concerning ground action. Headquarters, Naval Forces Far East, and Headquarters, Far East Air Forces, did likewise for naval and air activities, respectively. GHQ, FEC, in Tokyo, entered censorship operations only in the case of round-up stories or accounts rewritten after having once cleared. In such cases, the FEC censors considered only the material not previously evaluated.[24]

> As of 16 March 1951, all copy, even though it had already been censored in Korea, had to be submitted to the FEC censors' office for a final review.[25]

> At the same time, revised censorship criteria were issued to press and radio representatives as a strict guide. What was and what was not security information was no longer vague; and the conditions for reporting military operations were now specific.[26]

> To handle the final review of all reports, the FEC censors' office went on a 24-hours-a-day, 7-days-a-week basis. Army, Navy, and Air Force censors were always on hand to process material at any time it was submitted. A log was kept to prevent loss and to check handling time. Censors made no changes in the copy submitted, only necessary deletions. They did recommend revisions; and correspondents were always allowed to make necessary changes when deletions interrupted the continuity of their material.

> Still photographs, motion picture film, and taped radio broadcasts were subject to the same criteria as press stories. Photography received an additional measurement: Any photographs that could be recaptioned by the enemy for propaganda uses were banned. All tape recordings, the newest technique in combat reporting, were auditioned by censors. Where necessary, offending passages were snipped out.[27]

> The point of the January and March [1951] changes in censorship procedure was to achieve uniformity, an obvious advantage to both the press and the military. . . . The principal flaw in the system was that, with censors in both Korea and Japan looking over the same material, double censorship had been imposed. Correspondents in Korea justifiably complained

that the double check caused delays and also left them in the dark as to what further cuts had been made after their material left Korea.[28]

Censorship finally became a theater-level function on June 15, 1951. A single military censorship office in Tokyo, but with an operating detachment in Korea, handled all news stories. Direct telephone communications between the main office and the detachment were available. Both offices used the same criteria; "stops" and "releases" were uniformly applied; and all censors were uniformly trained in Tokyo. Meantime, the Eighth Army's role in the clearance process became an advisory one on tactical matters.[29]

No censorship of the mails had been imposed; commercial telegraph, radio, and cable facilities, all of which were available in some parts of Korea and all of Japan, were not monitored; nor were the Korea-Japan telephone circuits supervised. With regard to the latter, the Eighth Army chief censor had recommended in March that correspondents not be permitted to call in stories to their Tokyo representatives but be restricted to transmitting them over army-controlled teletype circuits. The recommended action was never taken. Hence, those correspondents who chose to evade the clearance process still had the means to do so.[30]

In addition, FEC censorship still could not prevent the disclosure of security information in reports prepared outside the theater, as the June 18, 1951, issue of *Newsweek* magazine made clear:

As Eighth Army Commander, both General Ridgway and his successor, Lt. Gen. James A. Van Fleet, had placed bans on the disclosure of the Eighth Army "order of battle" (the location and number of its major units). In an article describing a UN drive over the 38th parallel, the 18 June *Newsweek* noted the restriction: "Although censors cracked down on the identification of most U.N. units, they did clear broad hints that the victorious I Corps now comprised fighting men of eight nations, including three American divisions." But, ignoring its own reference to censorship, the magazine published on the same page a map of the battle area and the order of battle of I Corps.[31]

When General Ridgway pointed out this violation, *Newsweek* explained that the information had been compiled from cleared dispatches and other information which had been "promoted to the Pentagon for clearance and clearance granted. . . ." Department of the Army officials, however, advised General Ridgway that neither the article nor map had been submitted either to the Army or Department of Defense for clearance. *Newsweek's* next response was that it had compiled the order of battle by piecing facts together. The magazine [editors] seemed not to realize that printing order of battle information was a dangerous breach of security.[32] In an October 1951 issue of the magazine, the allied order of battle, this time of the entire Eighth Army, again appeared in map form.[33]

While both the Department of the Army and the Department of Defense had security review agencies to which such articles should have been submitted, no compulsory censorship existed in the United States. Department of the Army officials attempted to prevent security breaches such as that committed by *Newsweek* through repeated requests to the wire services and press that they publish nothing concerning the strength and order of battle of UN forces.[34]

In any event, *Newsweek* suffered no penalties for its breaches of the rules.

A new dimension in military-press relations arose in Korea near the end of 1951 as Western newsmen gathered at the Armistice talks at Panmunjom. Ironically, the Communists had initially objected to the UN proposal to bring twenty Allied newsmen and photographers to the conference area each day. Only after Admiral Turner Joy, the chief UN negotiator, refused to sit in further conferences until they gave in did the Communists yield. But late in 1951 the Western correspondents, according to the FEC public information officer, had entered into agreements with Communist journalists, namely Wilfred Burchett, an Australian correspondent for the French Communist paper *Ce Soir,* and Alan Winnington of the *London Daily Worker.* Specifically, the FEC public information officer told the FEC chief of staff then serving under General Matthew Ridgway that "The Associated Press made arrangements to smuggle a camera into its captured correspondent [Frank] Noel. Carefully screened pictures, exhibiting only smiling and well fed prisoners are then hand carried back. George Herman of Columbia Broadcasting, has challenged the censorship to stop the mailing by him of tape recordings or prisoner interviews, obtained by the same means."[35]

The public information officer urged the chief of staff in January 1952 to order the "senior U.N. delegate to the Armistice Conference to take all necessary steps to bar physical and vocal contact including the passage of articles or messages of any kind, between the correspondents accredited to the U.N. Command present in Panmunjom, and the representatives, in any guise, of the enemy." He also urged that any newsman who attempted to circumvent such a curb be permanently barred from the conference site.

The action taken to meet this problem was milder.[36] In February 1952, correspondents were admonished in a memorandum against inappropriate conduct while at the conference site. The matter apparently was not pursued further.[37]

There were two other instances cited in army records of violations of censorship rules or simple inaccuracies. In one case:

An American Broadcasting Company correspondent broadcast the erroneous statement that Gen. Ridgway "suffered recurrent heart attacks." He did not submit this statement to censorship and, even when informed that the statement was untrue, insisted that "this story is on the level." The broadcast prompted Washington authorities to inquire of Gen. Ridgway's health. Gen. Ridgway replied that he was in fine fettle.[38]

Throughout the conflict the FEC took few drastic steps against erring members of the press.* The press complained that there were several cases of news suppression, notably one that FEC public information officers found fully justified. This involved the riots in the Koje-do prisoner-of-war camp in the spring of 1952. No information was released on the grounds that publicity might make such information a factor in the Panmunjom armistice negotiations and might also adversely affect other military operations. When the information finally was released more than a month later, the story broke as an expose.[39]

There were delays, too, in the release of information concerning the prisoners' seizure of Brigadier General Francis T. Dodd, commander of the Koje-do POW camp, on May 7, 1952. For a brief time, in fact, no correspondents were permitted to visit the camp because of the tense situation that had arisen. One newsman, Sanford L. Zalberg, representing International News Service (although accredited to Reuters), managed to reach the island. He managed to stay eight hours before he was, in his own words, "firmly but politely" returned to the mainland. His story was held up for twenty-four hours, then, with the approval of his Tokyo bureau chief, was released as a pooler for all news services.

As it happened, when General Mark W. Clark replaced General Ridgway as UN commander-in-chief, he immediately instructed the Eighth Army commander, General James Van Fleet, to make a prompt and factual official account of all events and developments not only at Koje-do Island but at every POW camp under UN control.[40]

In the opinion of B. C. Mossman, in a 1966 report prepared for the Moss Committee (House Subcommittee on Foreign Operations and Government Information), the military-press relationship worked out fairly well. Not without avoidable red tape and administrative confusion, the military moved from an unworkable code of voluntary censorship to a compulsory review of press and radio reports.

---

* We find nothing in the record to support the assertion in *The First Casualty* (Harcourt Brace Jovanovitch, 1975) that General MacArthur expelled 17 journalists from Japan for criticizing his policies (p. 349). In his well-written, sketchily documented, widely read history of war reporting, the author, Philip Knightley, a British pacifist and London *Sunday Times* correspondent who never covered a war, contends that too many Western newsmen in Korea "became engrossed in describing the war in terms of military gains and losses rather than. . . trying to assess whether the [UN intervention] was justified. . . ." Mr. Knightley's assessment: "It remains difficult to name a single positive thing the war achieved" (p. 356).

In protecting vital military information, the censors actually applied only two basic measurements: (1) Would the release of a report offer aid and comfort to the enemy; and (2) would its release adversely affect the morale of UN troops fighting in Korea. As Mossman saw it, in spite of the fact that the inherently competitive nature of reporting and security requirements are natural enemies, most correspondents, especially seasoned ones, and the editors involved in covering the Korean conflict met the demands of censorship fairly. The FEC censors attempted to release the maximum of information.[41]

It is not surprising that there were so few complaints by newsmen. If anything, the military held back on enforcement of its own rules. When it came to a question of punishing newsmen for major security breaches that did occur, the military and its civilian superiors in Washington contented themselves with relatively mild rebukes: not even the publication by *Newsweek* of maps showing the (classified) location of U.S. units provoked official retaliation. As far as can be ascertained, no newsman was denied accreditation or lost it. Ironically, the best-known incident of temporary disbarment, that involving AP's Tom Lambert, in July 1950, did not involve security information; as we have noted, it followed Lambert's own (vain) request that uniform censorship be imposed to reduce the dangers of security leaks engendered by the competitive zeal of the wire services. And there were few protests by newsmen over censorship, once it was imposed; censorship, as we have seen, did not inhibit "news analysis," even of the gloomiest sort, or criticism of the military, which was routine. The horrors of war were not suppressed. Until the front stabilized in mid-1951, the chief complaints among newsmen concerned the chronic difficulties of communications and transport; later there were complaints over inadequate or misleading official UN briefings on the tortuous truce negotiations at Panmunjom. The inconclusive war became unpopular at home—an issue in the 1952 election—but neither General James Van Fleet nor other U.S. commanders in Korea later blamed this evolution on the security lapses, mood swings, exaggerations, or forebodings of the press.

· 4 ·

THE VIETNAM WAR

N O U.S. conflict since the Civil War was to stir so much hostility
among the military toward the media as the drawn-out conflict
in Vietnam. Indeed, some commentators (and generals) were
retrospectively to conclude that the war was lost on America's television screens and in the newspapers, not on the battlefield.[1] Spokesmen
for network television came to argue that journalists, especially television journalists, had brought the war home to the people, and that critics
were simply blaming the messenger for bearing bad tidings, for communicating unpleasant truths.[2]

To some degree, antagonisms between the military and the media
reflected a broader array of rising tensions that afflicted the United States
during the 1960s and 1970s. These confrontations arose as a result of
rapid social change amid unprecedented prosperity at home: civil rights,
urban riots, the anti-authority "cultural revolution" among the children
of the prosperous, and the erosion of consensus and self-confidence
among the nation's politicians, senior civil servants, college presidents,
businessmen, and news executives, who all faced challenges to their view
of things.

But the core of the military-press problem in Washington and in Saigon
lay in the central contradictions of the policies pursued by Presidents
Kennedy, Johnson, and Nixon.

It is fairly clear, in retrospect, that each president sought to avoid making Indochina the prime focus of U.S. policy. But each feared that no
U.S. president could "lose Vietnam" without adverse domestic political
repercussions, the loss of confidence of U.S. allies in Washington's commitments elsewhere, and the encouragement of Soviet aggressiveness
around the world.[3]

Thus the U.S. military was told, implicitly, by the White House to
avoid losing Vietnam—at the lowest possible cost militarily and politically.
(As Richard Betts has noted, the lowest possible cost kept increasing
and finally got too high.)[4] Especially in 1965-67, this ambiguous com-

mitment embraced the inherent contradictions of "guns and butter." It led to contradictions in administration actions and rhetoric as President Johnson incrementally sought to appease both "doves" (with bombing pauses and peace feelers) and "hawks" (with more troops, more bombing of North Vietnam) while assuring the general public that "progress" was being made in South Vietnam. The contradictions led to press skepticism well before the 1968 Tet offensive:

The Wall Street Journal, April 23, 1965: "Time after time high-ranking representatives of government—in Washington and in Saigon—have obscured, confused, or distorted news from Vietnam, or have made fatuously erroneous evaluations about the course of the war, for public consumption. . . ."[5]

Columnist Joseph Alsop, in a speech to the American Foreign Service Association, March 25, 1965: "An official is a man by definition doing the public's business. The public has a right, and the public has a need, to know about its business. . . . The truth is that practices have grown up in the American government in the last years—and particularly quite recently—of a kind that amount to an unseen and . . . extremely unhealthy change in the basic American system."[6]

Walter Cronkite, CBS News, speech to the Inland Press Association, Chicago, February 22, 1966: "I would like to suggest that one of the reasons for the great confusion which wracks this nation today over the Vietnam War is the fact that we were committed without a proper airing of the facts— all the facts. This administration and preceding ones did not level with the American people on the nature or scope of the commitment which, I submit, they themselves must have known was one of the ultimates [sic] of our policy."[7]

James Reston, *New York Times*, May 17, 1966: "What he [President Johnson] wants is worthy of the faith and confidence of the nation, but this is precisely what he does not have, because his techniques blur his conviction. . . . He is mixing up news and truth. . . . He is confronted, in short, with a crisis of confidence."[8]

Since the administration lacked a coherent strategy and clear-cut objectives (other than not losing) but claimed "progress," its spokesmen could not define for either the military or the public what ultimate "success" would require. As outsiders, not insiders, newsmen are often right for the wrong reasons—and when they were right in Vietnam, this was usually the case. They widely assumed that there *was* a coherent strategy, and that "progress" (in killing enemy troops, pacifying the countryside, strengthening the South Vietnamese ally) was intended to further this strategy. Newsmen in Saigon concentrated on the agenda set by the White House. They sought to check in piecemeal fashion the claims of "progress" made by official spokesmen—and often disputed privately in conversations with trusted reporters by U.S. military commanders and advisers to the South Vietnamese in the field. As military historians have later noted, the better journalists dug up solid information that the White House did not want to see in print for domestic political reasons.

Because both John F. Kennedy and, especially, Lyndon Johnson were extremely sensitive to "negative stories," even accurate ones, the strong reactions to the press coming from the White House or Pentagon down the chain of command tended to convey the impression to many senior military men (and diplomats) in Vietnam that the press and television were reporting home *only* "negatives" unfair to U.S. troops—and overblown negatives at that. Especially in 1965-67, the Johnson administration insisted that the military commanders—and military spokesmen—join the civilian leadership in promoting and defending administration policy and countering "negative" news stories. General William C. Westmoreland, the U.S. commander in Vietnam (1964-68), for example, was twice summoned home by LBJ to "sell" the administration policy to Congress and the press—an unprecedented use of the military to achieve domestic political objectives.

The relationship between the newsmen and the military public affairs people in 1961-68 was contaminated by U.S. domestic politics, as it had not been in Korea (for the most part) or in World War II. In the view of some critics, Presidents Kennedy and Johnson and Defense Secretary Robert S. McNamara sought to put the best public face on every aspect of the limited American effort, partly to avoid having to "bite the bullet" and make truly radical, politically costly decisions about U.S. involvement.

Most print reporters did not take the daily official communique-cum-briefings in Saigon ("the Five o'clock Follies") too seriously. Based on hasty, fragmentary, inevitably inaccurate field reports, the Follies were essentially the latest model of similar, on-the-record briefings and communiques that the military provided to newsmen during the Korean War, World War II, and World War I. Since the Vietnam fighting (except at Tet 1968 and during the 1972 Easter offensive) was mostly a seemingly disconnected episodic affair, with no moving battle lines, the Saigon communiques usually read like "police blotters," a daily compilation of seemingly random, small-unit engagements that in World War II or Korea might not have seemed worthy of notice; very often, for lack of other drama, the bombing raids against the North occupied the wire services' "lead," although no journalists were permitted to accompany the aircrews.

What the communiques were designed to do was provide the wire services (and hence radio, television, and newspapers) with a daily "hard news" story: Something Happened. This daily story, from official sources, dominated the Page One news from Vietnam as well as newscasters' studio reports on television and radio. That the Follies often turned into a spokesman-baiting exercise was less a matter of keen-eyed journalists challenging official "lies" or claims of "progress" than of venting the journalists' underlying frustrations over their inability to answer independently the question from the home office: "Are we winning or losing the war?" Thanks to years of official optimism (notably from Defense Secretary McNamara) that proved unfounded, newsmen in Saigon were inclined to discount *all* optimistic assessments by official spokesmen, even as they dutifully reported them.

Yet, ironically, in no previous American war was the press so well treated. General Westmoreland provided at least his rear-echelon troops (the majority of the 500,000 men under his command) with an extraordinary array of stateside amenities (including base-camp swimming pools, televised baseball games, cold beer, hot showers, and post exchanges filled with stereo sets), perhaps as compensation for the lack of a "win-the-war" strategy. Newsmen had access to all the amenities enjoyed by rear-echelon military officers. In addition, the U.S. Mission in Saigon provided "dedicated" spaces on in-country air transport and major press camps in each of South Vietnam's three outlying military regions, with telephone communications and daily flights to Saigon.

As time went on, helicopters in some army divisions were on occasion assigned exclusively to bringing reporters to units in the field; elsewhere newsmen could often hitchhike aboard helicopters or fixed-wing aircraft almost as easily in Vietnam as they could gain rides aboard passing jeeps in World War II. The helicopter peculiarly suited the fast in-and-out desires of television crews (although the three-man crews were more dependent on public affairs officers for assured transport than were individual print reporters); with luck, they could get to the scene of the action, get some "good film," and be back in Saigon or Da Nang the evening of the same day to get the film on its way to America.

All in all, during the period of the heaviest U.S. engagement in Vietnam (from 1965-72), journalists were coddled by the U.S. military in ways that often astonished their French and British colleagues.

The numbers of U.S. journalists (and foreign journalists) greatly increased as U.S. troop commitments increased. In 1964, there were only about forty U.S. and foreign newsmen in Saigon. By the summer of 1965, there were more than 400 (accredited). The Military Assistance Command Vietnam (MACV) was conducting daily briefings for 130 correspondents. As of August 27, 1966, there were 419 news media representatives accredited from twenty-two nations—179 were Americans, and dozens of foreigners worked for American media.[9] This figure was misleading; it included support personnel, nonresident newsmen, and wives of newsmen. Relatively few American journalists, perhaps forty in all, were in the field with U.S. troops (and even fewer with allied troops) at any given time, except during the rare periods of sustained combat, such as Tet 1968.

On July 14, 1965, the U.S. Mission in Saigon issued certain guidelines for correspondents on the "release of combat information." Among other things, the rules banned:

(1) Casualty reports and unit identification related to specific actions except in general terms, such as "light, moderate, or heavy." (Overall casualty summaries would be reported weekly.)

(2) Troop movements or deployments until released by MACV.

(3) Identification of units participating in battles.

With respect to combat photography and television, it was emphasized that visual close-ups or identification of wounded or dead, and interviews of wounded (without prior approval of a medical officer) should be avoided, out of respect for the feelings of the next of kin or the wounded man's right of privacy.[10]

There were relatively few violations of the ground rules by newsmen in Vietnam in 1964-68. Barry Zorthian, a former U.S. Mission spokesman in Saigon, observed in March 1983 that:

In the four years (1964-68) that I was in Vietnam with some 2,000 correspondents accredited . . . we had only four or five cases of security violations . . . of tactical military information. Our leverage was the lifting of credentials and that was done in only four or five cases and at least two or three of these were simply unintentional errors on the part of the correspondent. There was only once or twice that [ground rules] were deliberately challenged, and the correspondent's credentials were immediately lifted.[11]

There were violations that were not followed by a lifting of credentials. One involved a young *New York Times* reporter during the 1968 Tet offensive who reported in detail the frank briefing by the commander of the First Cavalry Division (Airmobile) on his unit's difficulties with logistics, helicopter availability, and other problems during the battle for Hue.[12] Other reporters had treated the general's briefings as off-the-record, in light of the ground rules and the tactical situation. The *Times* man was reprimanded by MACV but not otherwise punished.

John Carroll of the Baltimore *Sun* did temporarily lose his MACV accreditation in July 1968 for reporting the abandonment by the marines of the once-besieged outpost at Khe Sanh. Fellow correspondents protested and got the suspension reduced. Said an army historian, William M. Hammond, later: "I think the main reason MACV wanted the closing of Khe Sanh kept secret was [to save] face." Neither the Pentagon nor the Saigon headquarters command wanted the North Vietnamese to be able to claim (inaccurately) that they had driven the Americans out of Khe Sanh.[13]

World War II-style censorship was considered in 1965 at the Defense Department's request. But it was ruled out at the urging of U.S. officials in Saigon, as Hammond later observed, because: (1) it was impractical, given the freedom of reporters in Saigon to travel to Hong Kong or elsewhere to file stories free of censorship; (2) there was no censorship in the United States and could not be without a declaration of war; (3) the South Vietnamese, hosts to the American forces, would have to have had a hand in censorship, and they had already set some unpopular precedents with their own press; (4) it was impossible to censor television film for lack of technical facilities; and (5) it was difficult to suddenly impose censorship during a war which had long been covered without it.[14]

The ground rules worked out after discussion with newsmen in Saigon were adopted instead. Under the Nixon administration, as U.S. troop withdrawals began, the South Vietnamese troops began assuming a greater role in major operations, notably in the 1970 invasion of Cambodia and, more importantly, in the ill-fated advance on the Ho Chi Minh Trail in Laos in 1971, where U.S. ground forces provided backup around Khe Sanh but did not enter Laos itself, U.S. bombers and helicopters supported the South Vietnamese troops. Increasing friction developed between U.S. reporters and the South Vietnamese authorities and MACV over curbs on the press.

For the first six days of the Laos operation in January-February 1971, dubbed Dewey Canyon II by the Americans and Lam Son 719 by the South Vietnamese, a news embargo was imposed by MACV. No U.S. correspondents were permitted in the operational area, and no reports were permitted on the operation during the blackout. Yet three news organizations carried stories under datelines outside Vietnam, breaching the embargo. There was much criticism of the blackout in Washington and New York. Replied Defense Secretary Melvin Laird: "When I'm talking about reducing casualties as Secretary of Defense, I'm going to support that kind of decision by our military leadership in Saigon."[15]

The Vietnam conflict posed certain problems in coverage, quite aside from those caused by occasional curbs on access or publication. Said CBS's Eric Sevareid, after a visit in 1966:

The really puzzling problem of reporting this war lies right with the nature of news and its processing. Distance lends excitement if not enchantment. The lens of the camera or the lead paragraph of the newspaper story are like a flashlight beam in the darkness. They focus upon what happens to be moving. All else ceases to exist, and the phenomenon focused upon tends to become, in the minds of the distant readers and viewers, the total condition.

So one small riot in Saigon suggests at a distance that all of Saigon is in an uproar. It's not. The shooting [the May 1966 factional strife] up in Danang suggests that all of Vietnam is collapsing into civil war. It's not.

Even if the news itself is not distortion, its effect is distorted. What we have not sufficiently developed in this business are effective and immediate corrective techniques.

For journalists, the physical facilities here, especially transportation, are the best that I have ever seen, and the military press officers, the best trained. The normal, inevitable, and necessary tensions exist between press and military, but the mutual trust here is certainly higher than it is inside the Pentagon.[16]

In *Dateline 1966*, published by the Overseas Press Club, CBS correspondent Morley Safer wrote:

This is television's first war. It is only in the past few years that the medium has become portable enough to go out on military operations. And this has raised some serious problems—problems, incidentally, which every network correspondent and cameraman in Vietnam is acutely aware of.

The camera can describe in excruciating, harrowing detail what *war is all about* [emphasis added]. The cry of pain, the shattered face—it's all there on film, and out it goes into millions of American homes during the dinner hour. It is true that on its own every piece of war film takes on a certain antiwar character, simply because it does not glamorize or romanticize. In battle men do not die with a clean shot through the heart; they are blown to pieces. Television tells it that way.

It also tells what happens to civilians who are caught in the middle of battle. It tells what happens to soldiers under the stress of the unreal conditions in which they live. American soldiers are not *always* 100 percent sterling characters, just as American policy is not *always* exactly what is right for the world or for Vietnam's smallest hamlet.

The unfavorable has always been reported along with the favorable—but television tells it with greater impact. When the U.S. blunders [sic], television leaves little doubt.[17]

Morley Safer was sounding a persistent mythic theme in public discussion by television network stars of their work during the Vietnam War—and a theme often picked up by their critics: television as ultimate truth teller. The television networks seldom showed the dead or the wounded. Nor, with a few much-publicized exceptions (including Morley Safer's own emotive narration of the burning of a hamlet, Cam Ne, in 1965), did the television people show American misdeeds in their nightly bits on the news shows. The fact was that with the notable exception of Tet 1968 and the 1972 Easter offensive—when the war came to the cities and outposts where the cameras were—television bureau chiefs were often bedeviled by the problem of attempting to deploy their scarce camera crews to remote locales where the prospects for vivid action film seemed most likely. (Print journalists could always get some kind of story: they did not *require* visual melodrama.) But action in Vietnam was unpredictable, for the most part. And there was never assurance that an American unit, deploying to find and fix an elusive foe, would actually make contact, or that a camera crew would be in the right place to film it.* As a result, the television people often had to settle for something less, an "aftermath" story or a "feature," given significance only by the narration of the correspondent. Yet many champions and critics of television apparently believe, to this day, that Safer was right, apparently without viewing the coverage.

One critic, General Westmoreland, charged that "television's unique requirements contributed to a distorted view of the war" being brought into the American home. "The news had to be compressed and visually dramatic, and as a result," Westmoreland stated, "the war that Americans saw was almost exclusively violent, miserable or controversial."[18]

Another commentator, Robert Elegant, focused on the impact of the television coverage, saying, "For the first time in modern history, the outcome of a world war was determined not on the battlefield, but . . . on the television screen."[19]

But as a matter of fact, as Lawrence Lichty notes, while about half of all the television reports filed from Vietnam were about battles and military action, most showed very little actual fighting. From August 1965 to August 1970, only about 3 percent of all the evening network news film reports from Vietnam showed "heavy battle" (defined as "heavy fighting, incoming artillery, with dead or wounded seen on the screen"); that amounts to only 76 "heavy battle" stories, out of more than 2,300

---

*In a comment on the chapter, Ed Fouhy, CBS Saigon bureau chief in 1967, disagrees: "This bureau chief did not feel that way. The military PIOs were forever inviting us to go along on operations which they felt were going to take their units in harm's way. A few of those turned out to be a 'walk in the sun' but most were not. This was true for both the army, which sent PIOs to Saigon to make the rounds of the bureaus before every major operation, and the marines because of their cozy press camp near the Da Nang River. They had a captive press corps with whom to share intelligence on coming battles. Finally there was another, an absolutely fail-safe way of getting action and that was to hook rides on medivac helicopter runs out of the major air bases. . . . Whenever there was a major engagement the dust-offs were sent to where the action was and I often sent crews and correspondents along on those runs."

on the air during those five years that included the Tet offensive. A study of Vietnam-related television news film stories from 1968 to 1973 found that only about 3 percent of the stories contained combat footage, and only 2 percent showed any dead or wounded. Much of the coverage actually dealt with the "aftermath" of battle or various "instruments" such as the newest military hardware.[20] Perhaps the best summary of what actually did appear most often about Vietnam combat in American living rooms, then, is Michael Arlen's:

> . . . a nightly stylized, generally distanced overview of a disjointed conflict which was composed mainly of scenes of helicopters landing, tall grasses blowing in the helicopter wind, American soldiers fanning out across a hillside on foot, rifles at the ready, with now and then [on the soundtrack] a far-off ping or two, and now and then [as the visual grand finale] a column of dark, billowing smoke a half mile away, invariably described as a burning Viet Cong ammo dump.[21]

John Mueller, author of the detailed *War, Presidents and Public Opinion* (1973) disparages the notion that TV news changed the course of history:

> It has been found that popular support [as expressed in opinion polls] for the Vietnam War was remarkably similar to that for the Korean War during the [time] period in which the wars were comparable. Levels of support were the same, trends were the same, and both wars were supported by much the same demographic groups.
>
> Of course Vietnam generated far more *vocal* opposition than did Korea, but this seems to reflect the vocalism of the intellectual Left far more than it represents a substantial change in opinion among the wider public.
>
> The similarity of popular support for the two wars suggests that television, a rampant fact of life during Vietnam but a mere infant during Korea, may not have been as vital a force in shaping attitudes toward Vietnam as is often supposed. War, after all, is a singularly unsubtle phenomenon, and the assumption that people will know how they feel about it only if they see it regularly pictured on their television screens is essentially naive and patronizing.[22]

Yet there is no question that televised coverage of Vietnam lingers large in the minds of senior military officers. Their perceptions of press and television performance have been transmitted down the line to junior officers. Although they generally talk of the "news media," they have made on occasion a sharp distinction between television and newspapers. For example, in a survey of 100 generals who served in command positions in Vietnam, Douglas Kinnard found unanimity on this matter as on no other, except on the abilities of the South Vietnamese army.

His survey results were as follows:

Newspaper coverage of the war was	Percentage of Responses
(1) Generally responsible, and played an important role in keeping the United States informed	8
(2) Uneven. Some good, but many irresponsible	51
(3) On the whole tended to be irresponsible and disruptive of United States efforts in Vietnam	38
(4) Other or no answer	3
Television coverage of the war was	
(1) Good for American people to see actual scenes of fighting about when they occurred	4
(2) Probably not a good thing because such coverage tends to be out of context	39
(3) Not a good thing, since there was a tendency to go for the sensational, which was counterproductive to the war effort	52
(4) Other or no answer	5

Not all the generals (Kinnard himself is a retired general) were critical of the media. A minority saw shortcomings in the military's reporting on the course of the war. Echoing the sentiments of several senior army officers expressed on other occasions to this writer, one general put it this way: "We placed too much emphasis on the positive, and were over-sensitive to criticism, while engaging in false reporting to cover up set-backs. This, in time, led to our losing credibility."[23]

We do not know whether reactions to the media of most of Kinnard's respondents were based on viewing network television news and reading newspapers after the officers came home or on letters received from friends and relatives during the officers' tours in Vietnam, or both.

In the view of Major General Winant Sidle (USA, ret.), spokesman for MACV in 1967-69, the tenor of most coverage in Vietnam became more favorable to the U.S. military after General Creighton W. Abrams took command, succeeding General Westmoreland in mid-1968:

> Westy liked to have press conferences; he liked to have backgrounders; he liked to get on television. I'm not knocking Westy at all, but it turned out in the end to be somewhat counter-productive.
>
> Now General Abrams took an entirely different view of this. He had no press conference the whole time I was there . . . (but) he spent literally hundreds of hours in one-on-ones with every significant newsman in Vietnam who wanted to talk to him.

The result, said Sidle, was "pretty good" coverage after March 1968 until "Vietnamization" and U.S. troop withdrawals began under President Nixon in mid-1969. Favorable stories outweighed the unfavorable, even on TV. "I think," he said, "most of us have forgotten that because it got bad after that and stayed bad."[24]

The contradictions of the 1969-73 Nixon policy for South Vietnam—pulling U.S. troops out of the war while negotiating in Paris with the Communists to obtain "peace with honor"—did not lend themselves to coherent journalism at home or in Saigon. A continuous cacophony of anti-war rhetoric and peace demonstrations dominated discussion in Washington and elsewhere in the country during these years, and both newspaper editors and television news executives increasingly devoted more attention to Paris talks and the domestic "Vietnam issue" than to what was happening, overall, on the battlefield. The Nixon administration, faced with a hostile Democratic congress, felt besieged, and showed it. Yet there was, by all accounts, far less effort by the White House and the Pentagon to sell the notion of "success" than had been the case under Lyndon Johnson or John F. Kennedy. The government was defensive and secretive—on the intensified bombing of Communist bases in Cambodia in 1969-70, for example—and the White House was increasingly paranoid, as the Watergate scandal was to make clear. But the Nixon administration was perhaps less manipulative.

As General Abrams once observed to this writer, for each American "the Vietnam War begins when you get here and ends when you go home." Thus, journalists' views of the war depended partly on when they were in it. The American journalists arriving after early 1969 were coming to Indochina from a home front that was in a state of frustration, demoralization, and war-weariness. Congress constantly threatened to vote an unconditional end to U.S. involvement. The casualty lists lengthened. There were few hawks left. Every move by the administration was controversial. There was increasing willingness in Washington and in the major media to believe the best about the intentions of Hanoi and the worst about the U.S. military, the South Vietnamese, and the behavior of U.S. troops. Two indicators were the year-long media attention given to the My Lai massacre, revealed in late 1969, and the credence given to the claims, later shown by CBS to be dubious, by Lieutenant Colonel Anthony Herbert in 1971 that he had been sacked as an army battalion commander in Vietnam because he reported war crimes. As for Hanoi, the Associated Press distributed occasional dispatches by Wilfred Burchett, an Australian communist who covered the war from Hanoi's side. And, in the absence of a U.S. declaration of war, U.S. journalists did not hesitate to seek admission to North Vietnam (a quest that began with *The New York Times*'s Harrison Salisbury's controversial visit in late 1966); a handful were admitted, along with American antiwar delegations, to Hanoi even during the 1972 Easter offensive. Critical reporting of the journalists' hosts was rare. No such tolerance was extended to the South Vietnamese.

In Saigon, some U.S. news organizations granted credentials as stringers during this period to American newcomers who were less journalists than advocates. For example, in June 1970, CBS fired one stringer who also worked for Dispatch News Service, an embryonic "alternative" agency. He and several colleagues had donned armbands to join a Saigon student demonstration against the war, and were arrested by South Vietnamese police.[25] In another case of participatory journalism, newly-arrived riflemen of the 196th Infantry Brigade, the last U.S. ground unit in Vietnam, refused to go out on patrol near Phu Bai, apparently after being told by a visiting American television crew that they might face danger from land mines. It made for good film, but the TV journalists stirred the ire of the army unit leader.[26]

In Saigon, the press-government strains thus stemmed largely from the differing sensibilities of newly arrived journalists (reflecting those of the home front) and those of the U.S. officials charged with carrying out Richard Nixon's Vietnamization program. The latter tended, naturally, to see success as within their grasp. The White House decision to pull out U.S. troops (in mid-1969) inevitably eroded the morale and discipline of American units still in-country: the much publicized "fraggings" and drug abuse (reflecting army troubles worldwide in these years) resulted. The American withdrawal, not pacification or the decimated Viet Cong, was *the story* as ABC News told its Saigon bureau in 1969—and so it was in 1969-71, with the exception of the 1970 Cambodia invasion and the 1971 Laos operation. In 1971, Saigon politics and President Nguyen Thieu's efforts to consolidate his power became *the* story, and the Saigon regime became increasingly resentful of the critical attention given its performance by the Western correspondents. In effect, Washington was saying: South Vietnam will be able to go it alone. The question the Saigon reporters were properly asking was: Is this Vietnamization working? Their generally negative observations, sometimes inspired by those of U.S. field advisers, further angered the South Vietnamese authorities, who sought to restrict American reporters' access to South Vietnamese units without much protest from U.S. officials.

During Hanoi's massive tank-led 1972 Easter offensive, in particular, South Vietnamese authorities bitterly rebutted Western reporters' accounts of the early defeats suffered by ARVN units. ARVN checkpoints for a time barred reporters' access to the An Loc front north of Saigon and, later, to the Quang Tri front north of Hue. At the same time, intense competition among U.S. wire services occasionally overrode the ground rules (as they had in Korea in 1950). The U.S. command disaccredited a UPI reporter for forty-five days for disclosing unannounced ARVN troop movements; later, the South Vietnamese officials lifted the credentials of the AP's chief correspondent for the same offense.

Yet, possibly because U.S. military prestige was less directly at stake (U.S. advisers, ships, and aircraft were involved, but the ARVN was doing the ground combat), both Colonel Philip L. Stevens' small public affairs staff in Saigon and the few U.S. advisers still in the field were remarkably candid about the ups-and-downs of the Easter campaign. They were not omniscient, but they helped to provide journalists with a Big Picture that the Thieu government was unable or unwilling to supply.

In the end, the Easter offensive provoked few of the high fevers that shook the media in Saigon and Washington during the 1968 Tet offensive—aside from some TV commentary and a *Newsweek* cover story ("The Spectre of Defeat"). Colonel Stevens told this writer in Saigon in June 1972, as the Communist tide receded somewhat, that he had, overall, no complaints about the accuracy or fairness of the coverage— despite the inevitable fog of war and all the friction in Saigon.

Why was this so? One can only guess. But one should first look at the White House. Prior to Tet 1968, the U.S. government's Vietnam information policy had been to allow access by any and all journalists to the war zone (if not always in 1961-62 to U.S. advisers and helicopter support units). The Kennedy and Johnson administrations constantly sought to show "progress" in Vietnam to sustain congressional and public support on the Right and Left for an always growing but always limited and ambiguous effort to preserve a non-Communist South Vietnam. This entailed varying efforts to manipulate (or rebut) newsmen's reporting from Vietnam with optimistic statements aimed at short-term political results. A "credibility gap" was inevitable.

When Hanoi's 1968 Tet offensive erupted against the cities in an un-precedented Communist show of strength, the news media, especially television, were overwhelmed. Although he had been warned in advance by Westmoreland of a major enemy effort, Lyndon Johnson had not warned the American people (or the press) of impending Big Bad News. The news media hastily portrayed the enemy attacks as a DISASTER, real or impending, for the allied cause in South Vietnam. Tet turned out to be a military setback for Hanoi and a severe blow to the Viet Cong guerrillas. Most journalists, especially TV journalists, did not correct their first impressions. They have been blamed for Lyndon Johnson's political troubles of February and March 1968. But the journalists did not *cause* the president's torments, in my view, although they may have aggravated them (as they aggravate most White House difficulties). By his lack of coherence and candor before Tet and his failure to take charge just after the enemy assaults, Lyndon Johnson suffered a self-inflicted wound—a political crisis in Washington that ended only with his March 31 announcement that he would not seek reelection.[27]

In contrast to the Tet offensive, the Easter offensive of 1972 was not preceded by an administration "progress" sales campaign or four-star promises that the beginning of the end was in sight. Second, the Easter offensive came as no surprise; from administration sources, the news media had explicit warnings that an enemy attack was expected. (Indeed, major news organizations ordered reinforcements to Saigon *before* the attacks.) And when the North Vietnamese attacks came, unlike his predecessor, Richard Nixon responded with decisive actions—dispatching ships and aircraft, bombing North Vietnam, mining Haiphong harbor, making a new peace offer. He took charge. No media malfunction or political crisis occurred. George McGovern, the Democrats' eloquent peace candidate, lost the 1972 presidential election that November by a landslide.

What Vietnam makes so clear is that ultimately, the president is the key figure in military-press relations. He is the commander-in-chief. The president must insist on reasonable access for newsmen and on reasonable candor and coherence. The relationship between the senior military and journalists in Vietnam was soured by White House demands for "positive" information to be provided to the press by the military showing "progress." Civilians in both the White House and the Defense Department were seeking to soothe Congress and public opinion at home. The careers of officers who cited problems or setbacks in the field were not enhanced. The ambiguities and contradictions of White House policy and its public expression in 1961-68 led, inevitably, to the demoralizing burden of a "credibility gap" shared by the military, and inherited (and widened) by the next administration.

Should U.S. troops again go into combat, the best tonic for media-military relations (to say nothing of public support) is a clear presidential strategy and a sturdy resolve on the part of the White House not to gloss over difficulties. Credibility begins at the top. It is possible to be confident without being deceptive. The president sets the tone. By his words and decisions he sets the agenda for the military and, indirectly, for the news media. If the president wants the trust of journalists and the public, he will protect the military from political pressures to make things look better than they are, or can be. And he and his generals must remember that they, not journalists, win or lose America's limited wars.

· 5 ·

THE FALKLANDS WAR: 1982

F ROM a distance, the British government's handling of the press and television during the Falklands War appeared the exact opposite of the policy pursued by the U.S. government during the Vietnam War. London's policy was limited access for journalists, censorship, no television coverage, poor communicative facilities, some deception, even a bit of disinformation. Of course, it was a very different war. And the United Kingdom has a very different tradition of government-press relations—with far less access granted to the press.

On April 2, 1982, Argentina's president, General Leopoldo Galtieri, after repeatedly hinting that he would do so, sent his troops to the Falkland Islands to occupy the virtually unfortified British colony—population 1,800—in the South Atlantic, 500 miles from Argentina and approximately 8,000 miles from the United Kingdom. The British dispatched an expeditionary force to retake the islands. On June 14, 1982, after a final British assault, the Argentinian garrison surrendered at Stanley.

It took the British, unprepared for long-distance conflict, until May 1 to get their ships to the Falklands and land the first commando units on East and West Falkland. During the month it took for the fleet to move south, there was frantic diplomatic activity involving the United States, Argentina, and Britain, among others, in a vain effort to find a diplomatic solution.

It seems that Prime Minister Margaret Thatcher and her cabinet were worried about the "Suez syndrome." They were afraid that, as time went on, British home front opinion would divide and morale would erode, undermining the war effort, as had happened during the drawn-out preparations for the ill-fated 1956 Anglo-French invasion of Egypt after President Gamel Nasser nationalized the Suez Canal.[1]

Moreover, the British military operation was a risky one; the Argentinians had modern aircraft (and the French Exocet air-to-surface missile), and they had built up a sizable 9,000-man garrison on the islands, backed at home by a 130,000-man regular army and a 19,500-man air force.

In fact, in terms of numbers, they enjoyed considerable superiority. The British were sending an austerely equipped force of approximately 4,000 ground troops, with a few Harrier aircraft, to fight 8,000 miles from home.[2] This was not a Vietnam-era American expedition, rich in logistics, communications, air power, fire power, and other amenities.

The Ministry of Defense's information policy, according to the permanent undersecretary, Sir Frank Cooper, was based on the assumption that "the public has both an interest in and a right to know about defense. But we do not regard these rights as unlimited."[3]

By one account, one of the most serious mistakes by the Ministry of Defense was to cease all background briefings in London between the time of departure of the task force in early April and May 11, when the fighting got under way in earnest in the Falklands. Faced with the Ministry of Defense's refusal to provide more information, British television and the London newspapers began using retired military officers to help describe what was probably going on in the Falklands; often other information published or broadcast was supplied by reports from Buenos Aires. The Ministry of Defense in effect left a vacuum that was filled by others.

But the press had not been totally excluded from the task force; the Royal Navy did embark newsmen. The problem was more complex. Privately, many officials in the Ministry of Defense later said that they were embarrassed about their own lack of planning and inability to manage the press and displeased with the low priority the press was given during the operation, particularly with regard to communications, transportation, and other simple logistics. There was no prior Ministry of Defense plan to accommodate newsmen (there were no Ministry of Defense plans for anything outside a NATO context). Some twenty-nine photographers, technicians, and reporters finally sailed with the fleet in April to the Falklands, after Mrs. Thatcher overruled military recommendations that only six be allowed to go. In the view of several commentators, what wound up hurting the government's information policy most was not secrecy, but bureaucratic ineptitude and delay.[4]

The prime complaint by the news media was not so much censorship, which they understood, as lack of coordination; when, for example, on Tuesday, May 4, the destroyer *Sheffield* was fatally hit by an Argentinian air-launched missile, the journalists aboard the ships off the Falklands were told that the story had been embargoed in England. Similarly, the story of two Harrier aircraft colliding in fog was held up by the civilian censors with the task force. But the details of these and other similar incidents were released by Defense Ministry spokesmen in London, angering the reporters at sea.[5]

Even though the facilities for the press at sea were limited by the austerity shared by all in the British expedition, more than 600 dispatches and fifty hours of broadcasting tapes were sent to London by the shipborne correspondents. Written copy amounted to over a half-million words. Five reporters on one ship, the *Invincible,* alone provided between 25 and 30 percent of the daily work load for the ship's communication center, which at a stage when it had a backlog of over 1,000 military messages for transmission, still sent off 4,000 words of copy a day.[6]

During the Falklands War, there appeared to be no clear guidelines for censoring or vetting news reports. The commanders of the Falklands expedition were specifically instructed "not to interfere with the style and content of press copy other than on security grounds," while news editors back home responded amiably to requests from Defense public relations personnel to remove certain references in stories in order to safeguard morale and minimize distress to the next of kin.[7]

What the censors with the task force and those in London did was something in between censoring and vetting in that they appraised the correspondents' copy and asked them to remove or rewrite certain passages. The trouble was that the censors did not do it with any consistency. However, although much information was delayed, there were only a few slipups.

The censorship was two-layered:

The . . . journalists who sailed with the task force were accompanied by seven censors or "minders" from the Defense Ministry, as well as by the military press officers attached to each unit. Their job was to ensure that no potentially damaging information was transmitted to London, and since this frequently led to suppressing or excising the names of servicemen or the revealing detail of military action, they were deeply unpopular with the journalists, to whom such material was their lifeblood.

At the Ministry in London there was another layer of supervision, to make sure that reports did not give aid and comfort to the enemy, or threaten the security of operations. Frequently the two sets of censors were at odds.

Thus some correspondents with the task force were told in very firm terms that there should be no reference to the raids on Stanley by Vulcan bombers. "You won't even be able to tell your wives or your children about the Vulcans when you get back," warned one press officer. That evening the BBC reported the ministry's announcement of the Vulcan attack, and the unhappy "minder" found himself confronted by a group of very irate reporters.[8]

. . . Sometimes the anger was even more justified. John Shirley of *The Sunday Times* filed a story which included the sentence "Only the weather holds us back from Stanley." This was changed without his knowledge to: "Only the politicians hold us back. . . ."[9]

Later, British reporters who had covered the Falklands War told a parliamentary inquiry that official briefings had ranged from erratic to purposely misleading. Robert McGowan of *The Daily Express* said that reporters had been told that casualties were "minimal" after one Argentinian bombing attack when, in fact, fifty British soldiers died.[10] As *The New York Times* reported from London:

> Reporters were also led to believe that Argentinian troops were starving and suffering from dysentery, although it was later learned that they were as well provisioned as British forces.
>
> Brian Hanrahan of the British Broadcasting Corporation said earlier that Admiral John Woodward, commander of the task force in the Falklands, had told reporters "it was his intension to cause as much confusion to the enemy as possible, and if there was any way he could use us as part of that attempt, he intended to do so."
>
> "We reached an agreement," Mr. Hanrahan said, referring to the early stages of the conflict, "where he was entitled to stop us reporting things, but we were not prepared to report things that were incorrect. . . ."[11]

On the other hand, unlike the Argentinians in Buenos Aires, the Defense Ministry spokesman in London, Ian McDonald, had announced bad news as well as good; for example, he promptly disclosed the loss of the destroyer *Sheffield.*

On one occasion, the Defense Ministry decided to withhold the fact that two helicopters carrying Special Air Service (commando) troops had just crashed on South Georgia in the Falklands while the island was still in enemy hands. Newsmen knew that a landing was imminent. McDonald was pressed to say whether the British task force had gone ashore or not. He paused, then told newsmen no, it had not. Strictly speaking, he would argue later, this was no lie. The SAS, being special troops, was not part of the main landing force, only attached to it. In any event, the SAS had crashed, not landed.[12]

The Sunday Times team noted:

> There were, however, occasions when the Ministry of Defense, while not lying directly, certainly misled journalists with the calculated intention of deceiving the enemy. The false impression that the submarine *Superb* was on patrol in the South Atlantic, when in fact she was limping back to Britain, was never denied; and prior to the landings at San Carlos, everyone was actively encouraged to believe that there would be no such operation—only a series of hit-and-run raids.
>
> [Sir Frank] Cooper [permanent undersecretary at the Ministry of Defense] later argued that this was entirely justified in the circumstances of war, but it also undermined his authority and influence with journalists thereafter.[13]

In overall terms, McDonald later told *The Sunday Times* of London's "Insight Team," he had set himself two apparently irreconcilable ground rules: never knowingly to lie, and never knowingly to endanger the safety of the task force. He was confident that he never broke either rule. But he bent the first a bit.

The media had another complaint. As *Time* magazine reported on May 17, 1982: "News organizations all over the world chafed at the lack of pictures of the fighting." American television news executives, accustomed to easy access to the visual drama of wars in Vietnam, Lebanon, and El Salvador, were particularly unhappy. "We're covering this war with excruciating difficulty," said Jeff Gralnick, executive producer of ABC's "World News Tonight." "It's the first major story in a decade in which the television has not had immediate contact. You hear about the fighting but you don't see it."[14]

As it happened, during the early period of the war the news organizations in London were reduced to repeating contrasting communiques from Buenos Aires and the Defense Ministry. Oddly enough, some 150 British journalists with cameras, lights, tape recorders, and notebooks, representing more than a score of British news organizations, were allowed by the Argentinians to cover (from afar) the other side of the story in Buenos Aires—part of a larger foreign media crowd totaling about 500.

In Britain, in May, as the ground fighting began in the Falklands, controversy grew over the coverage from Buenos Aires and from the battlefront itself by British journalists. As *Time* noted:

> In Britain journalists were feeling a different kind of pressure: growing accusations that they are letting down their side by taking a neutral stance and occasionally reflecting Argentina's versions of events. On May 5 Conservative M.P. John Page complained that the BBC was using phrases like "If we believe the British. . . ." Said Prime Minister Margaret Thatcher: "I understand that there are times when it seems that we and the Argentines are being treated almost as equals and almost on a neutral basis."[15]

As the debate went on, a *New York Times* correspondent in London, William Borders, wrote that it recalled the "similar furor in the United States during the Vietnam war."[16]

There were technical factors involved in all this. As *Newsweek* noted:

> One reason British coverage has been so evenhanded is that, despite the shooting, British correspondents have been able to continue reporting from Argentina. *The Sunday Times,* for instance, was able to run side-by-side pictures of grieving war widows in Portsmouth and Buenos Aires. In fact, the TV coverage out of Argentina has an advantage: the British broadcast crews aboard the task force ships have no facilities for satellite hookups and have to send their film back to London by ship. "Here we are in the electronics age," lamented one frustrated BBC executive last week, "and our film gets back to us at 20 miles an hour."[17]

*　　　*　　　*

A public affairs officer at the U.S. Naval War College, Lieutenant Commander Arthur A. Humphries, U.S. Navy, after studying the Falklands War, concluded:

To maintain popular support for a war, your side must not be seen as ruthless barbarians;

If you don't want to erode the public's confidence in the government's war aims, then you cannot allow that public's sons to be wounded or maimed right in front of them via their TV sets at home;

You must, therefore, control correspondents' access to the fighting;

You must invoke censorship in order to halt aid to both the known and the suspected enemies;

You must rally aid in the form of patriotism at home and in the battle zone but not to the extent of repeated triumphalism (i.e., the Argentinian a-victory-every-day policy);

You must tell your side of the story first, at least for psychological advantage, causing the enemy to play catch-up politically, with resultant strategic effect;

To generate aid, and confuse at least the domestic detractors, report the truth about the enemy and let the enemy defectors tell their horror story;

Finally, in order to affect or help assure "favorable objectivity," you must be able to exclude certain correspondents from the battle zone.

Now that the first South Atlantic crisis of the century has been through "Hot Washup," the PAO [Public Affairs Office] armchair quarterbacks can conclude all of those things that I have just said, knowing there will be flak damage to repair domestically in a free-information society. But, "Objectivity can come back into fashion when the shooting is over."[18]

After the 1983 Grenada incursion, *Newsday* columnist Thomas Collins suggested that Humphries' comments had provided a blueprint for the Pentagon's handling of the press and television. Humphries said that, as far as he knew, no one in high office had ever paid any attention to his analysis.[19] But, in at least vague terms, as Washington reporters noted, there was no doubt that senior American officials, including the chairman of the Joint Chiefs of Staff, found the British military's experience with the media in the Falklands a refreshing contrast to that of the U.S. military in Vietnam.[20]

· 6 ·

GRENADA

A T NINE A.M. on Tuesday, October 25, 1983, President Ronald Reagan told a hastily summoned White House news conference that the United States had begun a pre-dawn invasion—four hours earlier—of the island of Grenada to "protect our own citizens, to facilitate the evacuation of those who want to leave, and to help in the restoration of democratic institutions in Grenada."

At President Reagan's side was Prime Minister Eugenia Charles of Dominica, chairman of the Organization of Eastern Caribbean States (OECS), which had asked for the United States' help. "I don't think it's an invasion . . . it's a question of we're asking for support."[1] There ensued a brief, unruly question-and-answer period. But the president did not go into detail on ground operations on Grenada.

The story did not catch the journalists totally unaware. Grenada, with an estimated population of 110,000 and with twice the area of the District of Columbia, was to some degree already established as a news story well before the invasion. Granted independence from Britain in 1974, the island republic was still a member of the British Commonwealth. In 1979, Maurice Bishop and his Marxist-inspired New Jewel Movement had taken power in a coup from the eccentric, autocratic Sir Eric Gairy and his "mongoose gang" of thugs. Bishop established close ties with the Cubans and the Soviets. The Reagan administration criticized Bishop for failing to hold elections, for putting his foes in jail, and for bringing in hundreds of Cuban technicians. In March 1983, President Reagan showed photographs of the new Point Salines airport, charging that the Cubans were helping Bishop build a 9,000-foot runway to accommodate Soviet aircraft. In June 1983, Bishop visited Washington and was given a hearing by William P. Clark, then Reagan's national security adviser. No detente resulted.

Grenada did not get back into the news until October 1983. On October 12, Bishop was ousted by his colleagues, principally Bernard Coard and General Hudson Austin. On October 19, Bishop and five others—

including Unison Whiteman, Bishop's foreign minister, and Jacqueline Creft, his education minister and consort—were massacred by army troops after Bishop's supporters freed him from house arrest and staged a rally at Fort Rupert in St. George's.[2]

General Austin emerged as the apparent new strong man and declared a twenty-four-hour curfew. It was then that leaders of the neighboring mini-nations, already apprehensive, began to fear the worst and gathered first in Barbados and then in Trinidad to consider what to do.

Radio Havana denied any Cuban involvement, saying, "No internal split justified the physical elimination of Bishop."[3]

In Washington, the new situation and a possible threat to American medical students on Grenada prompted a session of a Special Situation Group, headed by Vice President George Bush, on October 20.[4] As a precautionary measure, the navy task force carrying a replacement unit of marines to Lebanon was diverted southward.

On October 21, during a golfing vacation in Augusta, Georgia, President Reagan and Secretary of State George Shultz held private discussions about the Grenada situation.

On the same day, the Eastern Caribbean leaders met in Bridgetown, Barbados, and appealed to the Reagan administration for help on an informal basis. A message sent to Shultz in Augusta from the OECS leaders meeting in Barbados reached him Saturday afternoon.

As *The Washington Post* reported later:

> The diplomatic cable, in which the OECS states were joined by Jamaica and Barbados, stated "their very strong feeling" that they could not respond on their own to the Grenada situation, Shultz said.
>
> Shultz shortly thereafter discussed the cable with the new national security affairs adviser, Robert C. McFarlane, who was in Washington. Bush had convened a National Security Council [NSC] meeting in Washington and Shultz joined in by conference call "to evaluate the situation and the information in the cable."
>
> "We shortly got the president up," Shultz said, and brought him up to date. Reagan spoke by phone with Bush and Secretary of Defense Caspar W. Weinberger, and "gave his own reactions," Shultz said.
>
> At 9 A.M. Saturday, Bush started another meeting in Washington and Reagan spoke with him again. Reagan and Shultz talked about returning to Washington but decided against it, Shultz said, because they feared a sudden change in plans would call attention to the crisis, which was then a secret known only to top administration officials.
>
> But the Beirut bombing early Sunday changed their plans, and Reagan rushed back to the White House. Later, the White House received a formal plea from the eastern Caribbean nations to intervene in Grenada.

Early Sunday, former ambassador to Costa Rica Francis J. McNeil and Maj. Gen. George B. Crist of the Joint Chiefs of Staff were sent to Bridgetown to hold talks with the Caribbean leaders. Throughout the afternoon and evening, they were in telephone contact with the White House, Shultz said.

Reagan tentatively decided late Sunday to lead the OECS effort and to commit American military forces. At that time, there appeared to be a "very uncertain and violent situation" threatening American citizens on the island, Shultz said.

Also, on Sunday, the international airport at Grenada was opened for two hours so American diplomats could arrive to speak with U.S. citizens, according to the White House. Despite the report of a top official at the medical school on the island that there was no immediate threat to the students, the diplomats reported they found them in "high anxiety" because of restrictions on their movements and the shoot-to-kill curfew, a senior official said yesterday.

On Monday, Reagan began reviewing the military plans for the invasion with the Joint Chiefs of Staff and Weinberger at a meeting from 2:14 to 3:30 P.M., Shultz said. Reagan made a "semi-final" military decision at the end of that meeting. At about 6 P.M., he signed the directive ordering the invasion. Ambassador McNeil returned from Barbados that day.

Key congressional leaders were immediately contacted and brought to the White House for an 8 P.M. session with Reagan. They included House Speaker Thomas P. (Tip) O'Neill, Jr. (D-Mass.), Senate Majority Leader Howard H. Baker, Jr. (R-Tenn.), House Minority Leader Robert H. Michel (R-Ill.), House Majority Leader James C. Wright, Jr. (D-Tex.), and Senate Minority Leader Robert C. Byrd (D-W.Va.).

Reagan was joined by Shultz, Weinberger, [General John] Vessey, presidential counselor Edwin Meese III, chief of staff James A. Baker III, deputy chief of staff Michael K. Deaver, presidential assistant Richard G. Darman, and congressional liaison Kenneth M. Duberstein.

The congressional leaders were told of Reagan's plans but were not given a timetable.[5]

The military planning for Grenada was "very telescoped" according to Defense Secretary Weinberger.[6] In essence, starting on October 20, the plan was by all accounts designed as a rescue operation—in and out—aimed at the medical students. Then, on October 24 it was changed into a rescue plus clear-and-hold operation, especially after the White House got the green light from the Eastern Caribbean leaders on October 22.[7] All four services were involved.

The Joint Chiefs were haunted by the failure of Desert One, the April 1980 helicopter/C-130 operation aimed at freeing the U.S. hostages held in Tehran. That failure was blamed, in part, on a shortage of backup helicopters (as well as lack of interservice coordination and training). This time, there would be plenty of muscle available.

Moreover, in contrast to White House "micromanagement" of the Iran exercise and White House micromanagement under Lyndon Johnson of the air and naval war against North Vietnam, the Reagan administration, in essence, told the Joint Chiefs what needed to be done on Grenada and let them figure out how to do it.[8] Indeed, initially, according to navy sources, Admiral Wesley McDonald, commander-in-chief, Atlantic, had proposed that the operation be simply limited to the marines with their usual navy backup.

The planned invasion was kept as quiet as possible. The first public announcement took place, as noted, on the morning of October 25, after the invasion had started.

Some hours after Reagan's news conference, Shultz, at a State Department news conference, explained the background and chronology of the United States' decision to intervene. Mostly in response to questions, he also briefly outlined bits and pieces of the action on the ground:

> Both airports at Pearls and Point Salines have been secured. The elements of the Caribbean task force, that is of the countries from the Caribbean, are at Point Salines; they landed approximately at 10:45 this morning. I think there are about 150 there now. The southern campus of the medical college near Point Salines has been secured. There are no reports of injuries to any American civilians. There are pockets of resistance in the St. George's area; I don't want to identify further precisely where, because there is an ongoing operation and the military people need to be able to conduct their operations secure from any such disclosure.[9]

The Reagan-Shultz announcements did not catch the major U.S. news organizations unaware that *something* was going on in the Eastern Caribbean, even as they were distracted by the truck bombing of the U.S. marine billet at Beirut airport in Lebanon two days earlier, with a loss of more than 240 lives.

The New York Times's Frank J. Prial had reported from Bridgetown, Barbados, on October 23:

> Two United States diplomats left Barbados today to visit Grenada at the invitation of the Government to look into the safety of United States nationals living on the island. . . .

> Throughout the day, Grenada's government radio broadcast statements that the island was calm but also warned that a "military invasion of our country is imminent."

The radio statement came a day after a 10-ship United States task force was diverted toward Grenada in what Reagan Administration officials described as a precautionary measure.[10]

The Washington Post's Edward Cody, usually based in Miami, had reported from Port of Spain on October 22 on the meeting of the Eastern Caribbean leaders to "consider sanctions against the new military government that would range from a trade embargo to endorsement of possible U.S. intervention."[11] The tough reaction to Wednesday's bloody military takeover was reinforced by reports from Washington that "two U.S. Navy task forces, totaling 21 ships with 1,800 Marines have been diverted toward the island. . . ."[12]

The next day, Cody reported from Bridgetown that Grenada's ruling military council had "placed its armed forces on alert and called up militia reserves in the face of what it said was an approaching threat of U.S. invasion. . . ." The *Post* editors put the story inside the paper.[13]

On October 24, Pentagon spokesmen acknowledged that the navy task force originally bound for Lebanon was "on station" near Grenada. In a story by its Pentagon correspondent Fred Hiatt, the *Post* reported:

The aircraft carrier USS *Independence*, with 90 warplanes aboard, and 15 other surface ships in its wake [sic] continued to operate near the tiny island of Grenada. . . . A Marine amphibious landing group, with five ships and 1,800 Marines, also is nearby.

Pentagon spokesmen said last night that they have no information about an Associated Press report from Barbados, about 150 miles from Grenada, that 50 U.S. Marines arrived in Barbados yesterday in a Navy transport jet. The spokesmen also said they knew of no plans for U.S. military action in Grenada but added that the United States is concerned and monitoring conditions there.

The new Grenadian government, a leftist military regime, has said that the United States would use the safety of U.S. citizens living there as pretext to invade and dislodge the revolutionary regime.[14]

The CBS "Evening News" had that story on Monday night at 6:30, with Sandy Gilmour reporting from Barbados. The White House denied that Americans were in any danger on Grenada but said that, as Principal Deputy Press Secretary Larry Speakes put it, "The situation remains unstable." At 6:07 the next morning (October 25), ABC News had the first confirmed report out of Barbados of marines landing at a Grenada airport (Pearls airfield).[15]

Such news reports—and the turmoil on Grenada itself—spurred a certain number of journalistic deployments. Bridgetown in Barbados, 150 miles from Grenada, became the major base. Each of the three major networks had at least one reporter and a three-man camera crew (sound man, cameraman, field producer) there. On Monday, October 24, the *Post*'s Edward Cody, *Time*'s Bernard Diederich, *The Miami Herald*'s Latin American editor, Don Bohning, Morris Thompson of *Newsday*, *Time* photographer Claude Urraca, and two Britons—Greg Chamberlain of the *Manchester Guardian* and Hugh O'Shaughnessy of the *Financial Times* of London—were discovering that the Grenada airport was closed to incoming traffic (although four chartered planes apparently made it in and out); they decided to take a boat ride. They chartered a small fishing boat and, by stages, journeyed from Barbados to Grenada.[16] They did not reach the island until noon on Tuesday—six hours after the invasion began—and were restricted by the PRA (the People's Revolutionary Army, Grenada's military forces) soldiers in St. George's, the capital.[17] Already on Grenada were several journalists who had not been expelled or jailed by the new military regime. One of them was Paul McIssac, a reporter for Pacifica Radio and *The Village Voice*.[18]

Until the invasion, it was the story of just another Caribbean "hot spot."

The Administration and the News

In essence, the Reagan administration—that is, the White House—decided to hold the Grenada operation as close to the vest as possible, even within the White House staff. President Reagan's chief of staff, James Baker, decided to exclude Larry Speakes, the principal White House spokesman, and his aides from the NSC planning sessions. Speakes did not learn of the invasion until just after it began.[19] And at the Pentagon, Michael Burch, newly named (but not yet confirmed) assistant secretary of defense for public affairs, was not informed until the night before D-Day.[20] At the State Department, John Hughes, the senior spokesman, was also informed on October 24.[21] Neither Burch nor Hughes told Speakes.

The White House "close-hold" was based on the theory that those officials routinely dealing with the press would be better off *not* knowing what was going on than knowing and having to lie to inquiring reporters in order to preserve the secret.[22]

Presidents had used this approach before. Pierre Salinger, President John F. Kennedy's press secretary, recalled that "I was not informed at all about the planning [for the abortive 1961 CIA-backed Cuban emigre invasion] of the Bay of Pigs. As a result I was in a very delicate and embarrassing situation with the press. I did go to President Kennedy and I told him that if I was not informed I could not do my job. Even if there were things I could not say, I had to know. The President took that very seriously [thereafter]. . . ."[23]

The "Speakes episode"—which was later to cause a week-long furor—
began on the day before the invasion, Monday, October 24, when CBS
reporter Bill Plante called on Speakes at the White House. In a
March 30, 1985, note to this writer, Plante describes the incident:

At about 4:30 on the afternoon of October 24, 1983, I received an unsolicited
call from someone I have known for many years and have reason to believe
was once deeply involved in intelligence activities.

This source told me point-blank that there would be an invasion of Grenada
the next morning.

I scoffed, saying that perhaps U.S. citizens would be lifted out, but that
a full-scale invasion seemed most unlikely.

The source insisted that elements of the Army and Marines would go
ashore the next day and take the island.

This is what caused me to go to Speakes. He wasn't immediately available,
so I waited outside his office for fifteen or twenty minutes. Mike Putzel of
the AP was also present, and when Speakes appeared, I put the question
to him in Putzel's presence because I wanted a witness. (I didn't tell Putzel
what I intended to ask in advance.)

I asked Speakes, "Is there going to be an invasion of Grenada tomorrow?"

His initial reaction was to laugh. I then explained that I'd been told by
a source that an invasion was in the offing, and also asked about reports
that U.S. military personnel had already been sighted on the island. I asked
him to check.

He went into his office. He later explained to me that he called [Navy
Captain Robert Sims, the NSC spokesman] and that Sims called [Rear Admiral John] Poindexter [the deputy national security adviser]. Speakes came
back out in another ten minutes or so and said: "Plante—no invasion of
Grenada. Preposterous. Knock it down hard."

Some other circumstantial evidence was noted that afternoon which pointed
to a possible invasion. I made a number of calls—but CBS did not use the
story that night.

The next morning [on D-Day], I came to the White House press room
before 6:30 and discovered that the senior press staff was already in. When
I saw Speakes, he just shrugged his shoulders and gave me a sheepish grin.[24]

Later, White House Chief of Staff James Baker, a former marine, said
that he decided not to inform either Speakes or David Gergen, White

House communications director, about the imminent invasion because "the element of surprise was critical and American lives could have been lost" if the invasion had been confirmed in advance.[25] But Baker said he was in favor of getting the press ashore late on D-Day.[26]

The pre-invasion secrecy was one issue, but it soon faded.

The decision to keep the press away from the initial operation was another issue—and it did not fade. By all accounts, exclusion was the express wish of General John W. Vessey, Jr., chairman of the Joint Chiefs of Staff. And it was contained in the hastily drafted operations plan submitted by Admiral McDonald and approved by the Joint Chiefs, which called for exclusion of the press during the initial fighting, which was expected to last one day.[27]

According to another account, General Vessey told President Reagan that the military could not easily carry out the Grenada mission unless there were no press and television along to worry U.S. commanders.[28] Resentment over perceived antimilitary bias in the media, particularly television, during the Vietnam War and the success of the British in controlling press access to the fighting in the Falklands in 1981 loomed large in military thinking.

Hence no arrangements were made to take along a pool of newsmen during the Grenada assault—a decision further reinforced by the reality that no arrangements existed to ensure that newsmen could be designated, accredited, and alerted in advance without hazard to the secrecy of the operation. However, no advance plans were made by the Joint Chiefs to accommodate such a "pool" even after the assault phase was over; no public affairs officers were involved in the planning, and hence could not argue for a follow-up press plan. In essence, the public affairs aspects of Grenada were left in limbo prior to H-hour.

In his "Operation Urgent Fury Report," dated February 6, 1984, to the Joint Chiefs, Admiral McDonald wrote:

> The absolute need to maintain the greatest element of surprise in executing the mission to ensure minimum danger to U.S. hostages on the island and to the servicemen involved in the initial assault dictated that the press be restricted until the initial objectives had been secured. The rescue of the hostages was completed on the second day and the island was then opened to the press. Thus, media participation in the operation was restricted initially based on the military assessment of the importance that the element of surprise played in the successful execution of the mission and the consideration for the lives of both hostages and servicemen involved in the operation. Exclusion of the press did not reflect a conscious decision at this level.

The initial assault on Grenada was a highly complicated, hastily mounted operation, and afterward, it became clear that it was fortunate that the enemy was not in the mood for serious combat. It was a modest affair in terms of the number of men, aircraft, and heavy weapons involved. Indeed, in size it amounted to little more than a battalion raid: two rifle companies of marines, about 400 men, shuttled by a dozen helicopters from the *Guam* to a field close to Pearls Airport, the seaside commercial airstrip in the northern half of the island; 700 men from the First and Second battalions, Seventy-fifth Infantry Regiment (Rangers) parachuted in from C-130s onto the uncompleted 9,000-foot runway at Point Salines at Grenada's south end;[29] a still-undisclosed number of commandos (usually described as Navy Seals) who went into St. George's in three separate teams, and whose objectives were the rescue of Governor General Paul Scoon, seizure of the Grenada radio station, and the freeing of political prisoners in Richmond Hill prison.[30]

Prior to H-hour, Navy Seal teams went in. One team checked amphibious landing sites near Pearls Airport (none was found, forcing the marines to shift quickly from a sea-borne to a helicopter-borne assault). Another Seal team was to scout out the Point Salines area, but all four men drowned in a mishap.[31]

The military operations were scattered, complicating command and control (further complicated by lack of compatible radio communications, the involvement of all four services, and inaccurate information). The crowded command post of Joint Task Force 120 was aboard the helicopter carrier *Guam*. Vice Admiral Joseph W. Metcalf III, commander of the U.S. Second Fleet, was the task force commander.

The Ranger units were flying in from Savannah, Georgia. The initial follow-up troops—two battalions of the Eighty-second Airborne Division at Fort Bragg, North Carolina—were flown in from Pope Air Force Base, North Carolina. The commandos and the Navy Seals were flown from still-undisclosed locations. The Air Force C-130 Spectre gunships were from Eglin Air Force Base in west Florida. The navy aircraft carrier *Independence,* with A-7 and A-6 fighter-bombers, provided the backup air cover from out at sea. The operation's eleven CH-46 transport helicopters and four Cobra helicopter gunships were provided by the marines aboard the *Guam.*

The marines were Battalion Landing Team 2/8 (Second Battalion, Eighth Marine Regiment, Second Marine Division) under Lieutenant Colonel Ray Smith, plus the helicopter squadron, five tanks, and support units. They had embarked for Lebanon, where 40 percent of them had already served one tour, on October 17 aboard *Guam* and four smaller ships from Moorehead City, North Carolina.[32]

On October 20, near Bermuda, their commanders were told to sail to a spot 500 miles northeast of Grenada. If they got no further word, they were to proceed to the Mediterranean. They had nautical charts, but no maps, of Grenada. Their officers contemplated, at most, a show of force or a swift evacuation of Americans. Not until midnight October 23 did they get plans and orders for Operation Urgent Fury.

Not until the evening of October 24, after meetings and (changing) plans at Commander in Chief Atlantic Fleet (CINCLANT) in Norfolk, Virginia, did Admiral Metcalf arrive on the *Guam* with his army deputy, Major General Norman Schwartzkopf, and a staff to set up his command post, barely eleven hours before the marine assault was to begin.[33]

All the dispersed U.S. forces had to be coordinated and brought into action on short notice with as little advance warning to the Cubans and Grenadians as possible. (No one in the Pentagon has yet explained why fifty U.S. servicemen [actually Admiral Metcalf's advance party bound for the *Guam*] landed at the airport in Bridgetown, Barbados, via navy transport jet and took off via helicopter on Monday, October 24, all in broad daylight, as reported that day by the Associated Press.)[34] Moreover, there existed no clear picture in Washington of the strength, weaponry, deployment, or cohesion of the Cuban or Grenadian military or paramilitary forces on the island. (Original estimates from the Central Intelligence Agency of the *number* of Cubans—some 600-700—turned out, after all, to be accurate.)[35] There were no tactical maps of the islands.

"We were not micromanaging Grenada intelligence-wise," said Admiral McDonald later.[36]

As set by the president, Weinberger, and the Joint Chiefs, Metcalf's mission was (a) to find and rescue over 600 American medical students at True Blue campus near Point Salines (intelligence did not know of the second campus at Grand Anse, closer to St. George's); (b) to rescue Governor General Paul Scoon; (c) to neutralize the Grenadian People's Revolutionary Army and secure the island.

Even as the military plan was necessarily improvised, there was, to repeat, no improvised plan or timetable to deal with the press and television. With the assent of their civilian superiors, the Joint Chiefs in Washington left that detail and most others up to Admiral McDonald and his man on the spot, Admiral Metcalf.[37] As he planned the operation, Metcalf set up a system of reporting to CINCLANT in Norfolk from the *Guam* twice every hour, summarizing fragmentary radioed reports (often inevitably erroneous) from the dispersed units on the island or from U.S. aircraft supporting them.[38] From these reports came the information that the Washington officials variously interpreted and reported to the press.

Later, talking with reporters in Bridgetown on October 29, Admiral Metcalf greeted them with handshakes and a certain number of contradictions. He accepted responsibility for keeping reporters out of Grenada during the first two and a half days of Urgent Fury, despite "enormous pressure from Washington," and yet called himself the reporters' "best friend." He said: "I want to get you there, but I'm going to insist that you can be supported when you get there."[39]

Long after the operation was over, Metcalf told a Naval Academy alumni meeting in San Diego that, if the Pentagon proposed it, he would have agreed to having a pool of eight reporters accompany his task force off Grenada, but he was worried about what effect a large contingent of of press would have had on the invasion. Then he got to the heart of the matter: "I did not want the press around where I would start second-guessing what I was doing relative to the press. I cannot duck the issue. I had a great deal to do with keeping them out. I think I did the right thing."[40]

By all accounts, amid hasty operational planning, neither Metcalf nor McDonald laid down any specific timetable to accommodate newsmen either on Grenada, in briefings on Barbados, or at the command post on board *Guam*. No communications, transport, or other support were earmarked in advance of D-Day for the press and television or for military public affairs officers. There was no public relations "annex" to the Urgent·Fury plan. Just as public affairs officials in Washington were left out of the planning, so were their military counterparts in Norfolk, Virginia.*

Captain Owen Resweber, chief public affairs officer for CINCLANT in Norfolk, was informed of the planning for a possible Grenada invasion on October 23, two days before D-Day.[41] He did not tell Michael Burch at the Pentagon. There was no order to Resweber from anyone to develop a public affairs plan, however, until Wednesday, October 26, according to Major Donald Black, U.S. Air Force, a CINCLANT public affairs staffer.[42]

However, CINCLANT did swing into action on the customary deployment of military audio-visual teams. On Sunday, October 23, CINCLANT alerted the air force's Colonel James Elmer, commander of the Aerospace Audio Visual Command, at Norton Air Force Base, California, to dispatch an eight-man audio-visual team from Norton and Charleston, South Carolina. (A second group of five came later.) The USAF team went to Pope Air Force Base, North Carolina, on Monday, October 24. They arrived in Barbados on October 25, D-Day, and went into Grenada the next day. Said Elmer later: "Our mission is to go in and document the operation for historical purposes. We treat virtually everything we do.as classified." It is up to higher authorities "to decide what to do with the material we send them."[43]

According to Captain Resweber, two six-man navy video teams stopping off at Barbados landed in Grenada, probably at Point Salines, on October 25 (D-Day), after the airport was clear. Two Marine Corps camera crews, already embarked with the marine landing team aboard

---

*To avoid accidents, Metcalf ordered U.S. navy ships and aircraft from the *Independence* to bar all civilian aircraft or shipping after H-hour from the Grenada area, perhaps not so incidentally frustrating several newsmen's efforts to come in by chartered transport.

Guam on October 17 en route to Lebanon, went ashore near Pearls Airport soon after the rifle companies did.[44]

In Washington, D.C., amid growing media complaints about being excluded from the Grenada scene and about the lack of Pentagon planning for journalists, Colonel Robert O'Brien, U.S. Air Force, deputy assistant secretary of defense for public affairs, kept in touch with Captain Resweber at CINCLANT in Norfolk, at the direction of Michael Burch, newly named but not confirmed as assistant secretary of defense for public affairs.[45] On Wednesday, October 26, Burch received permission from Defense Secretary Weinberger and General Vessey, after approvals by Admiral McDonald and Admiral Metcalf, to start preparations to accommodate the growing crowd of frustrated newsmen on Barbados. "They [O'Brien and Burch] asked us to put together a plan, which we did," said Major Black.[46] The final decision to dispatch an interservice public affairs team was made by Admiral McDonald late on Wednesday, October 26.

Resweber dispatched his deputy, Commander Ronald Wildermuth, U.S. Navy, and five aides, including Major Black, from Norfolk to Bridgetown, Barbados, to set up a CINCLANT Joint Information Bureau (JIB) in a building at the Grantley Adams Airport next to where a U.S. Air Force base detachment was controlling the shuttle of U.S. aircraft to and from Grenada. Wildermuth's group arrived at 10 A.M. on October 27. The JIB had no direct communication link to Admiral Metcalf or to the army command post at Point Salines. The U.S. embassy in Bridgetown could provide no assistance. To contact Admiral Metcalf's staff on the *Guam*, JIB officers had to go to the U.S. embassy in Bridgetown, telephone CINCLANT in Norfolk, and ask the staff there to contact the *Guam*. In this roundabout fashion, permission from Metcalf was secured early on October 27 for a press-television pool to go to Grenada later that day—after the medical students were evacuated. Wildermuth recalled what happened:

> First of all we went to the [U.S.] embassy [in Bridgetown] to find out if there would be a pool, and . . . we found out that there would be . . . approximately 15. We asked the embassy, since this was a joint operation, which media from the Inter-Caribbean [countries] should be included in the initial pool. And they told us that they needed six seats in the pool, so we gave those six seats to the Caribbean media that they selected. [Of] the remaining seats, . . . the philosophy was that we would select the organization, the news media organization, and the news media organization would select who goes. Our policy was to give [the seats to] a representative from each one of the [television] networks including CNN, and then some kind of a pool crew made up of one sound man and one cameraman. And also an AP and UPI representative and a Reuters representative from the [foreign] media. And then some kind of a photographer to do color and black and

white. Our philosophy was to get the most coverage we could from the number of people we were allowed on the aircraft.[47]

On Thursday, October 27, the first newsmen to go to Point Salines airfield from Bridgetown included three Caribbean reporters (at the urging of the U.S. embassy in Bridgetown) as well as twelve Americans.*

The three major wire services and the four major television networks were represented, including one camera crew (CBS) that was supposed to share its product with the rival networks. There were perhaps 370 journalists at Bridgetown with varying professional credentials. At first, according to Wildermuth, the journalists tried to organize a pool among themselves:

> It was absolute pandemonium. I had reporters crawling over the wall. . . . What we did was go out there and say, "We have this many seats, we want to take these organizations, and have you select the person from that organization that will go and have him report to us with credentials." And that seemed to work fine. In fact, we got very little resentment from the media after they understood that we were there to help them expeditiously get over to the island.[48]

A check was made of individual press cards, but no new separate accreditation was issued. There was considerable tumult.

When the first press group arrived at Point Salines airstrip at 1 P.M., they were greeted by Commander Tony Hilton, U.S. Navy, from Admiral Metcalf's staff, who had helicoptered back and forth from the *Guam* since D-Day. Captain (now Major) Barry Willey, U.S. Army, had arrived only that day, following up the Eighty-second Airborne Division troops, and found himself without communications, transport, or command guidance on how to deal with newsmen. More than forty-eight hours after the U.S. assault, the last students had just been evacuated; St. George's was secured by the marines; Cuban arms warehouses had been discovered; but the Rangers were involved in some sort of firefight with Cuban and Grenadian holdouts near Calivigny Barracks, east of Point Salines.

Captain Willey took the newspeople on a carefully guided group tour. He did not know them well; no procedure had been set up for them to go very far; no troops or transport were available to get them around

---

*Members of this pool consisted of people from Associated Press, United Press International (photo), NBC, NBC Video/Audio, CBS, ABC, ABC Video/Audio, Cable News Network, Reuters, *U.S. News & World Report* (reporter and photographer), Caribbean News Agency, Caribbean Broadcasting (three).

the island or to the units in action; the busy Ranger unit leaders had no time to waste on outsiders; the Eighty-second Airborne Division commander was similarly preoccupied.

Was the press pool itinerary planned in advance? Captain Willey later said:

> Yes, I guess it was. We determined that they would be interested in seeing the immediate area around Point Salines airstrip and some of the important aspects of the operation including the captured weapons warehouses and the prisoner compound, some enemy vehicles that had been knocked out at the end of the airstrip. It was not feasible at that time to take them very far away from the airstrip area.[49]

Said Commander Wildermuth:

> That first day when we were finished with the media tour, . . . we allowed the media to interview students and even some U.S. AID people who were there, more or less interviews of opportunity. They couldn't talk to the Cuban prisoners. But we were held up two hours [in returning] the first day because of military action around the airport.[50]

Hundreds of journalists had gotten to Barbados before the CINCLANT public affairs officers set up the JIB. ABC's Steve Shepard was among them:

> Along with journalists from many other organizations, I arrived in Barbados on a commercial flight on the night of Tuesday, October 25 [the night of D-Day]. As the plane taxied to the terminal, I got my first glimpse of U.S. military activity in the region . . . a number of C-130 transports, clearly marked with USAF insignia, lined the ramp. Parked nearby were military versions of the DC-9 . . . also in Air Force livery. As my flight was disembarked, ABC ENG crewmembers Bobby Freeman and Joe LoMonaco attempted to videotape the parked aircraft and the dozens of U.S. military personnel both on the airport rampways and inside the Barbados civilian terminal. They were instructed by American military officials to stop taping immediately. Just moments after my arrival in Barbados, it had already become clear that covering the Grenada invasion was not going to be easy . . . that U.S. military authorities weren't going to be cooperative.
>
> Later that evening at the Sandy Beach Hotel where ABC News had established a headquarters, producers Sharon Sakson and Steve Schnee informed me that the two airports on Grenada had been closed to civilian traffic by U.S. military officials and that Barbados ATC wasn't allowing pilots to file any flight plans with a Grenada destination. They added that American and Caribbean authorities had declared an exclusion zone around Grenada . . . no civilian aircraft or boats would be allowed within thirty miles of the island. . . .

Sakson and Schnee had . . . persuaded a local charter service to sail in the direction of Grenada Wednesday morning and, if possible, land a mixed ABC-ITN [Independent Television News] London television team. ITN correspondent Brent Sadler, along with ITN cameraman Mario Zannini, were selected to join ABC Radio correspondent Tim Ross, ABC freelance sound man Doug Abbott and me for the 120 mile trip.

Most of Wednesday morning was spent provisioning the boat. The charter captain also spent several hours getting written authority to depart the port of Bridgetown and filling out the required customs forms. To the best of my knowledge, our departure from Barbados Wednesday afternoon was entirely legal.[51]

After stopping off at Union Island, part of the nation of St. Vincent and the Grenadines, Shepard and his companions headed for Grenada's Carriacou Island (they were in fact following a route earlier traced by *The Washington Post*'s Ed Cody, *Time*'s Bernard Diederich, and *their* companions). The navy was alert. They were spotted by navy aircraft and an A-6 Intruder bomber—the Viking dropped a cannister directly in the path of Shepard's boat, and the A-6 seemed keen on enforcing Admiral Metcalf's ban on civilian shipping. Shepard turned back:

Two days later, on Saturday, I traveled with the [third] group of journalists to be flown by the U.S. military on an officially sanctioned trip to Grenada. Upon arrival at Point Salines Airport, we were welcomed by Admiral Metcalf. Metcalf told us in so many words that we'd not been allowed on Grenada earlier because he had no way to get us there, because he couldn't feed and provision us and because he couldn't guarantee our safety. The assembled journalists responded that we were willing to get ourselves to Grenada, take care of our own food and lodging and take our chances with security. It didn't make any difference. We got to Grenada by military transport and took guided and supervised tours or we didn't get to Grenada at all.[52]

His ABC colleague, Mark Scheerer, came in, too, and later reported:

Upon arrival at Grantley Adams Airport, Barbados, Tuesday evening [October 25] around 9 P.M., Elyse Weiner, Tim Ross and myself found the tarmac area off-limits to reporters. Observation deck, open to public, forbidden to photographers and video crews. U.S. military personnel walking around main terminal wouldn't talk; no officers or spokespeople accessible. A quarter-mile west of main terminal is old terminal, site of Airlift Command Center (ALCC). Access through gate at that end of airport is denied to media. Apart from setting up TV cameras outside fence on nearby bluff and shooting with telephotos at planes coming and going, there's little reporters can do.

On Wednesday morning, [October 26] with number of arriving journalists and crews climbing toward 300, the four pay phones in the front, or outside part, of the main terminal have waiting lines. . . . Still photographers are having their film confiscated and video crews are chased off observation deck. . . .

Around 8 P.M. a representative from Barbadian Prime Minister's office meets with journalists in an airport office, apologizes for mistreatment, takes names for possible pool flight to Grenada Thursday, and conducts not-for-taping briefing which reveals Barbadian government knows little, tells less.

Barbadians *do* want media coverage of the departure of 60 Royal Barbados Police officers for Grenada, which has been promised all day Wednesday. Around 9, about 15-20 reporters, including myself, Mark Potter and ABC crew, are led onto tarmac for first time. Ordered not to videotape by Barbadian police, crews continue to do so surreptitiously, and I ROSR [reporter's on-scene report] the scene. Grenada-bound Barbadian Police never show up (they eventually embarked the next morning) and Barbadians lead reporters right to the ALCC, where men, machinery and supplies are in transit. . . .

U.S. Air Force officials, startled to find herd of reporters in the midst, go bonkers and threaten to confiscate film and tape. Potter leaves with a videocassette under his shirt, I stash audio cassettes in my underwear and duck through a door to another part of the off-limits area. I find an empty office with a phone and feed ROSRs and FYI to New York. . . .

Thursday morning an Air Force public info officer arrives, a Joint Information Bureau is set up, a media room is opened, telephones are ordered, and a pool of 14 reporters sent in on a tight tether. Military spokesperson says they [journalists] have been told to share their info and tapes on return. . . .

A briefing with Brigadier General Robert Patterson of the [Military] Airlift Command is promised Thursday, pushed back repeatedly, never materializes.

When Dick Threlkeld returns Thursday night with the pool, I feed his ack and ROSR, then return to press room to find other radio reporters screaming at CBS's Sandy Gilmour who won't share his audio, claiming no such pool was agreed to. An Air Force P.I.O. also screams at Gilmour, promises radio guys he'll make it up to us on Friday's pool list. We are told later that Pentagon complained to CBS and CBS rebuked its correspondents in Barbados. CBS is represented on Friday's pool list. Mutual and AP Radio are added, ABC Radio denied. AP Radio correspondent yields his place to AP writer. UPI Audio correspondent left off list, also. Friday's pool grows to 24 individuals overall. I'm pulled out, returning to Ft. Lauderdale Friday afternoon, via ABC-charter Lear Jet.[53]

The Wall Street Journal's Thomas E. Ricks got into Barbados on October 25:

On the day of the invasion, I was flying into Miami to write about Eastern Airlines' labor relations. I was on a Pan Am flight to Barbados within half an hour of hearing of the invasion and getting the word to go. It was the first flight to Barbados after word of the U.S. action got out, and was of course packed with reporters and film crews. . . .

Barbados officials weren't prepared for the influx of journalists. For the first couple of days, neither they nor the U.S. officials at the airport made any effort to accommodate the small crowd of reporters milling around in the airport lobby.

Toying with the idea of writing about the press (the foreign desk wasn't interested in it), I wrote this: More than 20 military aircraft and helicopters crowd the tarmac. U.S. Navy jets fly in and out. Americans in fatigues stroll around the runway, servicing equipment and moving cargo. They wave at an incoming Pan Am jet, but they do not respond to the shouted questions of reporters. The journalists are frustrated. The military men here won't talk. The embassy here, such as it is, refers all questions to the State Department. There are no briefings, no press releases, no nothing. Some television cameramen have been sitting here in the airport for six days. They talk half-seriously of storming the barricades. . . .

By late Wednesday the press was plenty pissed off. And tense: those of us with limited budgets or wise foreign editors sat in the airport and watched *Newsweek* and CBS charter planes for outrageous amounts so they could drop reporters and photographers all over the Caribbean and try to sneak into Grenada. . . .

For whatever reason, after a couple of days, the [U.S.] authorities opened up a press center in the old airport terminal. At first it was just a hot room with a few metal chairs, but they soon installed about 30 phones, and by week's end, were handing out free beer.

. . . Competition was fierce for the following day's [October 28] pool. It was difficult to get through to the U.S. military flacks in the airport—they ventured out from behind closed doors only to announce the pool—and the crowd of journalists was growing every day. By Friday morning, there were a few hundred clamoring to be on the plane. I had assumed I'd be on the Friday plane, and was shocked to see I wasn't. . . .

I was first on the list Saturday, which was a better trip because the military was allowing longer trips and more territory. (I have the impression that the first pool, and perhaps the second, basically saw the airport in Grenada, and the warehouses.)

We landed Sat., Oct. 29, at 1:15 P.M. We were herded into the un-completed airport terminal, where Vice Admiral Joseph Metcalf stood on cement steps. One of the first questions was about his exclusion of the press. (I think that by this point Weinberger had hung it on him.) He responded: "The point is, I've got a tough job here. We're trying to get this place cleared (my handwriting is bad here: he might have said 'cleaned') up. As soon as we can get sanitation, get a place for you to stay, then the press will be allowed in." (That statement, of course, was nonsense. There were no sanitation prob-lems on the island. Nor was there a food shortage, which had been invoked as an earlier excuse—we have to be able to feed you. I ate better on Grenada than I did on Barbados.)

Metcalf was so [impossible that] I wandered away to interview the grunts sitting around. Whenever I did, I got a "Can't talk about it."

So I wandered back to Metcalf, who was saying, "We've been shooting at boats. I don't know if there's press on them. We haven't sunk any."

Metcalf struck me as kind of high, almost hysterical. The flacks then marched us out and split us up into two groups of, I think, about 15 each. We weren't told why. It turned out that our group, stuck in a pretty dirty dumptruck, was being taken to the same stupid warehouses about a mile up the road that the pool had seen the previous day. This meant we wouldn't see anything new. Tempers rose, but at least we were on Grenada, and the military guys said as much. The flacks then told us the other group was helicoptering up to St. George's. Not only might there be a story there, but they got a chopper ride. Charlayne Hunter-Gault of PBS-TV was especially peeved: they'd split her away from her film crew.

That's about what happened. As we stood around, a crack of a rifle shot—the soldiers said it came from the hillside above—sent everybody scamper-ing into a warehouse. Choppers were called in to circle the erring hillside. We were led to another [Cuban arms] warehouse. . . .

From the warehouse we went to see the Cuban prisoners. When we got there, we saw about 60 (?) guys sitting on the cement, surrounded by con-certina wire. The flacks said "First rule, no Cubans." We couldn't talk to them. So I went to talk to Grenadians. Others followed. Bereft of her own TV cameraman, Charlayne Hunter-Gault tried to get the guys from SIN, the Spanish U.S. network, to film a standup. She said they screwed it up.

At 6 P.M. we took off for Barbados.[54]

According to the chronology of significant events compiled after Opera-tion Urgent Fury by the JIB, Admiral Metcalf flew over from Point Salines to Barbados at 8:30 P.M., Saturday, and briefed the newspapermen who had not gone with Thomas Ricks and the rest of the pool that afternoon.

On that day, the JIB director in the St. George's area, Commander Wildermuth, while accompanying newsmen, repeated his request of the previous day (to CINCLANT) that Metcalf's headquarters fly a briefing officer over from Grenada daily to update the press at the JIB at Bridgetown.[55] It did not happen.

The Magnitude of the Coverage

All told, the JIB sent 24 newspeople (including *The New York Times*'s Michael Kaufman and reporters from other major newspapers)* to Grenada for a guided tour on Friday, October 28, with advice on selection from the U.S. Embassy and the Pentagon, and 47 more on Saturday, October 29, with Ricks; and 182 (with no restrictions, at the behest of the White House) on Sunday, October 30. On November 1, the JIB opened an office under Major Douglas Frey of the Eighteenth Airborne Corps (parent unit of the Eighty-second Airborne Division) in the Grenada Beach Hotel near St. George's. The Rangers had already departed, and the marines were about to depart for Lebanon. But more than 100 newsmen daily went to Grenada aboard air force aircraft until November 4, when Wildermuth left for his home base at Norfolk.

There were, by JIB count, 369 American and other foreign journalists of one sort or another in Bridgetown, Barbados, on October 27. This total roughly matches the number accredited to General Dwight D. Eisenhower's Supreme Headquarters Allied Expeditionary Force in May 1944 prior to the Normandy invasion—in which only twenty American reporters accompanied U.S. assault forces onto the beaches. It was larger than the number of American journalists accredited to General Douglas MacArthur's headquarters in Tokyo early in the Korean War. And it is considerably larger than the total number of Americans accredited to the Military Assistance Command Vietnam on March 1, 1968, during the Communist Tet offensive—and many of those accredited were, in fact, either supporting staff or newsmen usually based elsewhere in Asia. It is considerably larger than the first press and television group (twenty-two journalists) that covered the action that followed the U.S. intervention in the Dominican Republic in April 1965.

On a practical level, what did this sizable influx of journalists mean?

---

*The pool consisted of reporters from Associated Press, United Press International (two), *Newsweek* (two), PBS, CBS (three), NBC, ABC, Cable News Network, BBC, Mutual Broadcast Radio, Scripps/Howard, *Time,* Voice of Barbados, Jamaican News Agency, *The Washington Post, The New York Times, Los Angeles Times, The Washington Times,* Time/Life photography, Spanish Radio Network.

It meant, in part, that the Grenada operation, or rather a journalistic base for the Grenada operation, in Bridgetown, Barbados, was close enough to the United States (in this case, Miami International Airport) to make coverage relatively easy and inexpensive—compared to, say, coverage of the Persian Gulf or Beirut.

The influx also signified the readiness of major news organizations to deploy their manpower for a dramatic short run story if not for longer running developments.*

By December 1983, the Associated Press Caribbean news editor, Dan Sewell, was reporting in the *AP Log* that "The international press corps that reached more than 400 has dwindled to a dozen Caribbean specialists." A withdrawal, he said, "that accelerated after the last official news briefing in St. George's on November 23, 1983."[56]

To some degree, all U.S. news organizations must deploy "fire brigades" of reporters who can cover any kind of a story. But these "fire brigades" are not necessarily well-versed in the American way of war. Nor, it should be added, are those newsmen routinely assigned to the Caribbean, although a number of them have learned on the job in Honduras and El Salvador to deal with the Latin military and U.S. military advisers. All armies are not alike, just as all football teams are not alike; in this case, the press corps deployed to cover Grenada, by all accounts, had only a few reporters along who had had previous prolonged contact with the U.S. military. And it showed in what coverage did take place.

The wire services, faced with supplying news twenty-four hours a day, were the biggest and fastest of the print organizations. The Associated Press foreign editor in New York, Nate Polowetsky, dispatched Kernan Turner from San Juan to Barbados on October 24, along with Caribbean news editor Dan Sewell. Then came New York reporter Rick Pienciak (who tried and failed to get into Grenada by fishing boat) with a half-dozen photographers and photography stringers. (United Press International had no record of its deployment for Grenada.) *The New York Times* eventually sent four reporters from the United States to Barbados. *The Washington Post* sent two. Unlike the wire service people, at least half of these reporters had had some prior experience covering the U.S. military. *Newsweek* sent three reporters and several photographers. (One female reporter and one photographer managed to get into Barbados by boat on D+3, tagging along with Eighty-second Airborne troops advancing from Grand Anse toward St. George's.) *Time* magazine dispatched one veteran reporter, Bernard Diederich, who had covered the 1965

---

*Scores of newsmen, notably network television people, went to El Salvador for the March 1982 elections; there was a sharp drop thereafter in numbers of reporters and in coverage of the running story. The Grenada story followed this pattern.

Dominican Republic invasion, by boat to St. George's; he arrived there in company with Edward Cody of *The Washington Post* and others six hours after H-hour. Diederich and two colleagues stayed on Grenada while Cody and three others hastened out to the *Guam* aboard a helicopter, hoping to file their stories from the command ship; instead, they came under eighteen-hour sequestration.[57] *Time's* other reporter who went to Barbados was Caribbean news chief Bill McWhirter out of Miami, who had covered wars in the Middle East and in Vietnam. (It is worth noting that the *Time* magazine Grenada stringer, Alistair Hughes, was arrested after the murder of Prime Minister Bishop, but his release from jail was arranged by Diederich on October 26.[58] Hughes also filed for the Associated Press.)

The big deployments were made by the television networks, each with twenty to thirty-five people going to San Juan, Havana, and the rest of the Caribbean.[59]

Most of these people were the servants of technology. Each network correspondent who appeared "on camera" was normally accompanied in the field by two or three others: a cameraman (using videotape) with twenty-five pounds of equipment, a sound man with a forty-pound recorder, and perhaps, a field producer. Support personnel in Barbados swelled the total.*

Thus, the buildup in Barbados for television far exceeded that of its big-league counterparts in print. At one point in the Grenada story, ABC's chief coordinating producer, David Green, was coordinating four or five two-man camera crews, six correspondents, four field producers, four tape editors, plus other helpers, as many as twenty-six people in all. Why so many camera crews? The networks now must produce news for both morning and evening and late-evening news shows—they are becoming more and more like the wire services with their own two "news cycles." And the producers want a variety of camera shots to choose from.

As military public affairs officers are well aware, technology has changed the whole approach to television's overseas coverage. Vietnam, it is said, was television's first war, but the technology was primitive. Television news crews went into the field with three men: reporter, cameraman, sound man. The equipment was bulky. Film had to be flown from Saigon to Tokyo or elsewhere in Asia for processing before being sent by satellite or airplane to the United States; most picture coverage

---

*For ABC's five correspondents in Iran during the hostage crisis in 1980, there were five producers, five two-man camera crews, a business manager, two expediters, and five other helpers—twenty-three people, or more people than made up the entire *Washington Post* overseas staff at the time. See Michael Mosettig and Henry Griggs, Jr., "TV at the Front," *Foreign Policy,* no. 38 (Spring 1980), p. 76.

of the war was at least twenty-four hours old before it reached the television screen. Back in Saigon, the correspondent, in effect, could throw his film and his script in a bag and go out to dinner for the evening once he got back from the battlefield. This is no longer necessarily true.

Now portable videotape cameras eliminate film processing, and satellite ground stations (if available) mean that television crews can transmit quickly and around-the-clock via satellite to New York. The videocassette material can be edited on portable machines (although this adds 800 to 1,000 pounds of equipment to the news team's load). All this adds to the complications of television coverage. Given the intense competition among the networks, extraordinary pressure is put on the correspondents and producers in the field for speedy creation and transmission of video stories to New York for both morning and evening news shows, especially when the story is hot.

In many respects the difficulties of eyewitness press coverage were not much more grave in Grenada than those on other occasions when U.S. forces have launched amphibious or airborne attacks. As has been noted, the news of the Normandy invasion, for example, did not come from reporters on Omaha Beach, most of whom were unable to get their dispatches back to London for several days, but from SHAEF in London. Similarly, the first intervention by marines in the Dominican Republic in April 1965 to rescue U.S. citizens and restore order was largely reported from Washington via official announcements; press access was delayed by local circumstances, not by U.S. policy, and by the end of D+1, the U.S. Navy helped to get the first group of twenty-two reporters from San Juan, Puerto Rico, to Santo Domingo, where, amid a civil war, no U.S. restrictions were put on their movements.[60] Explicit curbs were in force during Operation Delaware during the Vietnam War (April 19, 1968); in fact, a ten-day embargo was then imposed on all news of the operation, and no reporters accompanied the First Cavalry (Airmobile) Division assault forces by helicopter into the Ashau Valley, close to the Laotian border. Journalists were allowed to come in shortly after the landing sites were secured. That operation involved two army brigades—far more troops than were initially involved in Grenada.

The chief problem in Grenada was both an attitude and a lack of planning by the Pentagon and the White House.

A Better System

Had a public affairs annex to the Urgent Fury plan been devised, presumably CINCLANT would have established a joint information bureau at the Bridgetown airport some time early on D-Day. Then, as the Eighty-second Airborne Division battalions went in after the initial assault by the Rangers at Point Salines and the airport was secured, a public affairs team could have accompanied the Eighty-second Airborne troops and spent the afternoon and night getting ready to receive a press pool on D+1. At the same time, the joint information bureau in Barbados could have arranged briefings and transportation.

This fairly routine plan would have required a designated C-130 transport and, possibly, extra communications between Point Salines and Bridgetown. Had all this been done, in the opinion of some military public affairs officers, with the benefit of hindsight, perhaps the twelve-man pool that was sent in on October 27 could have come in to Point Salines from Bridgetown, Barbados, on the morning of D+1, that is, October 26. Some press and television coverage of several major centers of U.S. activity on the island would then have been possible.

However, one serious problem, obvious from both the Washington pronouncements and military after-action reports, was that the Joint Task Force-120 command post, with its superior communications, remained aboard the *Guam*. There was no central headquarters on the island itself; each element reported separately to the admiral's staff aboard the *Guam*. Hence only a (presumably smaller) pool of newsmen brought to the *Guam* could have gained any notion (assuming they were kept informed) of the Big Picture, since all elements in Joint Task Force-120 were widely dispersed and separated. If newsmen had been briefed on the *Guam*, they would probably have had access to certain details that got lost in the Pentagon. But the Big Picture they could have conveyed would not have been either complete or unflawed. It would, at best, have been based on fragmented reports from the green field units and military reconnaissance aircraft. Inevitably, these reports were often in error, notably in tending to exaggerate enemy strengths and opposition expected or encountered. There was also the tendency, on the part of some commanders at least, to identify all their opponents during the first day or two as Cubans. This confusion was reflected in the reports sent to Washington from the *Guam* and in the information made public by the Pentagon.

Aside from the practical difficulty of obtaining accurate and comprehensive information, newsmen at Point Salines would probably have been confined to the airstrip area on D+1, as they actually were on October 27. At 4:00 P.M. on the 26th, the Eighty-second Airborne battalions were still approaching the surrounded medical students near Grand Anse Beach. The Rangers went in aboard marine helicopters at Grand Anse Beach to pull out the students. If newsmen had been present on Point Salines airstrip, they would have seen the students being brought in from Grand Anse aboard the marine helicopters and being transferred to aircraft for the lift home. But they would not have seen the marines operating in St. George's against meager resistance. They would have seen two more battalions of the Eighty-second Airborne coming in at nine o'clock that night (D+1) to reinforce the army troops at Point Salines.

The pool that did get to Point Salines late on the 27th did not observe the fight at Calivigny Barracks, a training area where Soviet and Cuban advisers had reportedly been training the local Grenadian militia. The same Ranger battalion (Second Battalion, Seventy-fifth Infantry) that had rescued the students at Grand Anse the day before was put into the battle at Calivigny. The attack on Calivigny Barracks began in mid-afternoon. As B. Drummond Ayres later reported in *The New York Times*,[61] Eighty-second Airborne troops surrounded the barracks area while navy guns and fighter bombers pounded it. However, during one air strike, a bomb fell in the midst of some paratroopers, wounding twelve. Admiral Metcalf put in the Rangers. According to a Ranger platoon leader, First Lieutenant Raymond Thomas, the Rangers were plagued by mishaps as well. "We were told there were 30 Russians and 400 Cubans . . . that it was almost a suicide mission," Thomas said later, reflecting the general Joint Task Force-120 exaggeration of enemy strength. The Ranger battalion commander sent his three rifle companies straight into the camp. The first Black Hawk helicopter came in too fast, landed too hard, and bounced into a ditch. Two more close behind it crashed when a pilot took a bullet through an arm and a leg. His aircraft lurched into the one beside him and the two choppers crashed. It was here that all three of the Second Battalion fatalities occurred as well as the bulk of the unit's twenty-eight other casualties. Fifteen men were injured. After all that, the Calivigny Barracks was virtually deserted. "We didn't find anything worth shooting at," Thomas said.[62]

The press at Point Salines did not see firsthand either of those mishaps on October 27, nor were they informed of them, possibly because public affairs officers did not know of them and once again, the central command post was out aboard the *Guam*, where word of the mishaps was sent from the units involved. Whether, in the hypothetical pool suggested, newsmen could have been transported to and from the units in the field two or three miles away from Point Salines remains problematical, although on D+1, the 160th Aviation Battalion, which flew the Black Hawk helicopters, came in from Fort Campbell, Kentucky. Some helicopters might have been available on D+2.

In any event, it is important to remember that under such surprise circumstances, with both military and press thrown together as strangers in a strange place, with little advance planning, the military are likely to be cautious. They fear newsmen getting shot by friendly fire or by hostile action as well as the problem of civilians simply getting in the way.

There was no clear idea either among press or among the military of what they would encounter on Grenada. Both military and press, in essence, deployed "green" troops: the military were persuaded by prisoner interrogations and reports of "Cubans" for a time that there was a sizable Cuban combat-ready contingent on the island.[63] The Rangers, according to *The New York Times*'s Drummond Ayres, did not know beforehand that there was a second group of students at the Grand Anse dormitory. The Rangers had not been briefed on that fact. Reinforcements poured in—the third and fourth battalions from the Eighty-second Airborne plus other units, after word began to spread that resistance was stiffer than anticipated and that a prisoner had said there were 1,100 Cubans on the island in all—most well-trained. As senior army officers later acknowledged, this was a hasty assumption. The military were erring on the side of caution throughout, partly because they had so little sense of what was really going on.

In the Dominican Republic, Korea, and Vietnam, to say nothing of World War II operations, the military and the press had time to get used to each other, to establish at least some sort of modus operandi. In Operation Urgent Fury, a suddenly mounted exercise under austere conditions provided no warm-up time. There was, less excusably, no guidance to public affairs officers, no arrangement to handle a press pool, and not much clear information available in any one place at any time during the operation. It is noticeable, for example, that the few press wrap-ups that were done were not written by reporters who got to Grenada on October 27 and during the next few days partly because the best sources had already departed; they were done later by reporters, with experience of the military, in Washington.[64]

The chronological accounts in the November 7 *Time* and *Newsweek* magazines were based heavily on Pentagon briefings, according to Defense Department sources. This was at least in part because no reporters had access to Admiral Metcalf's central command post staff on the *Guam* and no knowledgeable Joint Task Force-120 staffer came to Barbados or Point Salines to supply an overall viewpoint, at least the overall viewpoint garnered from the messages reaching headquarters.

To some extent, *Newsweek* and other news organizations did not pay close enough attention to the significance of the low casualty figures, which were announced as early as October 30 as sixteen killed (in action or in accidents), seventy-five wounded, and one missing in action (on October 31, the final count was given as eighteen killed in action, eighty-six wounded, and one missing in action).

Newsweek's account made it sound as if the battle was much fiercer than it was in reality. The Cubans were described as having at least half a combat regiment on the island of Grenada.[65] *Time* magazine was more skeptical. According to the Associated Press, United Press International was perhaps the most imaginative of all. On Friday of Invasion Week, October 28, the *AP Log* later reported "an acrimonious scene" developed during a session with presidential spokesman Larry Speakes at the White House. At one point Speakes waved a copy of a bulletin filed by United

Press International about a supposed 1,000 Cubans fighting in the mountains. Speakes said it was erroneous:

> The first story out of there was just as wrong as heck. . . . It indicated there was a major fire fight going on. It brought about 15 of you up here in my office and . . . it said it involved 1,000 Cubans.
>
> This fellow had 1,000 fighting around Port Salines Airport. It was totally erroneous.
>
> The point was the reporters went in—the [UPI] guy who covered the war and saw it personally came out with a bum story. The AP got it right.[66]

Another problem for the press on the island was that the troops of the two initial assault units who could have provided more eyewitness detail were either off the island or on their way out five days after D-Day—the marines and the Rangers. Most of the troops encountered by the reporters once the constraints were lifted were GIs who had nothing to do with the initial assault. All of the Rangers, for example, were out by the end of October 29.

The circumstances of Grenada were peculiar. They were extremely unfavorable to either good coordination or planning. By one estimate, mishaps were responsible for almost half of the American deaths and a fourth of the wounded in the operation.

This reflects less on military efficiency than it conveys the fact that resistance was light and scattered after the first day. To the troops dodging snipers' bullets this would not seem so, but by normal battle standards it was not an arduous exercise. In retrospect it might be said the Rangers were lucky that all 600 of the Cubans were not, in fact, either determined to fight or militarily competent and that all the anti-aircraft weaponry found near the Point Salines airfield was not put into use.

It must be added that the Reagan administration in Washington created a backlash of skepticism by insisting too strongly during Invasion Week on what could only have been at that point a tentative assumption: that Cubans were getting ready to take control of the island.

And hence, high estimates of the Cuban presence got the benefit of the doubt in official statements, and the fact that Grenadian troops suffered by far the larger number of officially recorded enemy casualties was not emphasized. It is not clear to this day why Grenadian troops and/or Cubans did not take the medical students hostage at Grand Anse or why more Cubans fought or did not fight in the vicinity of the airport. To the Ranger officers, all the initial fire was "Cuban," at least when they spoke later to newsmen. That some Cubans did fight seems clear. Exactly why they were fighting and what they intended to do remains unclear. The U.S. government did not extend itself to provide information concerning this and other matters to reporters in Grenada, even after the operation's first few days.

Many questions remain. What was the role of the Cuban ship *Vietnam Heroica* (which remained off St. George's Harbor through the whole invasion)? Why did the Cubans bar the airport area to all Grenadians, as was reported, just before the invasion? Why did the U.S. commandos have so much trouble the first day in St. George's? Why were the radios of the various services incompatible? Why did U.S. forces not have maps? Why did Admiral Metcalf order in a second brigade of the Eighty-second Airborne Division? The Reagan administration did not volunteer the answers. Oddly enough, the press and television seem to have devoted more of their energy to agonizing over why they were excluded than on redeploying their manpower and seeking to piece together the full story during the weeks that followed Urgent Fury.

· 7 ·

PRESS FREEDOM: RHETORICAL AND CONSTITUTIONAL ISSUES

T HE seeds of a government credibility problem and a press-military controversy were planted when, the day before the Rangers landed at Point Salines, presidential spokesman Larry Speakes said in response to questions from reporters that the idea of an invasion of Grenada was "preposterous."[1]

At a news conference on October 26, the day after the invasion, he was faced with a confused, angry group of White House reporters trying to catch up with foreign reports and get the story straight. Pressing for details on the invasion their colleagues on Barbados were not allowed to see, Washington reporters stressed that they were among the few who knew nothing of the impending invasion.

> *Reporter:* For the record, you have told us that Radio Grenada was shouting to the world that they were about to be invaded, so the element of secrecy does not—surprise doesn't seem to be too strong here.

> *Reporter:* The only people who were surprised by this were right in this room.[2]

Speakes, as discussed earlier, was not directly to blame for misleading journalists. The White House had decided to keep its spokesmen in the dark so that they would not be in the position of having lied to the press. This strategy was not unanimously endorsed. As reported in *The Washington Post*: "Some officials acknowledged that the White House may pay a long-term price for, as one of them put it, 'advertising that our press officials just aren't told what is going on.'"[3]

The White House decision to pass on misinformation and to exclude reporters from the action on Grenada contributed to the page-one *Washington Post* headline "Invasion Secrecy Creating a Furor."[4] Defense

Secretary Caspar W. Weinberger and General John W. Vessey, Jr., chairman of the Joint Chiefs of Staff, in an October 27 press conference, offered the following reasons for the restriction. First Weinberger stated:

> The reason [for the exclusion] is of course the Commander's decision, and I certainly don't ever, wouldn't ever dream of overriding Commanders' decisions in charge of an operation like this, their conclusion was that they were not able to guarantee any kind of safety of anyone including of course anybody participating and that you have to maintain some kind of awareness of the problems going into areas where we don't know what kind of conditions totally will be encountered. Where the airport was obviously heavily overloaded with all kinds of activity and we just didn't have the conditions under which we thought we would be able to detach enough people to protect all of the newsmen, cameramen, gripmen, all of that.
>
> As soon as the Commanders notify us that it is appropriate, and I hope it can be as soon as tomorrow, newsmen can go in.[5]

A reporter then said that risks were always a factor and that the airfields had been cleared "since the earliest hours," to which Weinberger replied:

> Well, we didn't have anything much beyond the airfield secured and also there's a lack of knowledge, and as we encounter various unexpected pockets of resistance or pockets of resistance that are stronger, why then you do have that worry and while it may not seem credible to some of you it was indeed the concern that we had for the safety of newsmen and media, television as well as radio and print media.[6]

Vessey added:

> I think one of the most important reasons that we didn't [work with the press] was the need for surprise in this operation. We were going in there very quickly and we needed to have surprise in order to have it be successful.[7]

The press was not receptive to the explanation. When Larry Speakes stressed the aspect of the journalists' safety, ABC's White House correspondent Sam Donaldson said, "Don't tell me Ronald Reagan has our safety at heart!"

Speakes replied, "Why are you so venomous?"

"I'm not venomous but I'm insistent that what you're doing here is covering up," Donaldson said.[8]

Rhetorical Issues

As early as October 26, the day after the invasion, media representatives were protesting the news restrictions.[9] Television reacted quickly on the 26th, broadcasting commentaries and interviews such as John Chancellor's "NBC News Commentary":

> Well, there's one thing you can say about the invasion of Grenada; it isn't a living room war.
>
> There are American troops in combat, fighting with Cubans, putting Russians into custody—and not a single member of the American press allowed to observe.
>
> The American Government is doing whatever it wants to do in Grenada without any representative of the American public watching what it's doing. No stories in your newspapers or magazines, no pictures in your living room.
>
> When the British went into the Falklands they allowed a few correspondents and cameramen to go along, a small tip of a hat to a free press. But in Grenada, the Reagan Administration has produced a bureaucrat's dream: do anything, no one is watching.[10]

Donaldson offered a strong personal assessment on ABC's "Nightline":

> I think there's a deliberate effort by this White House and the previous White House to mislead the press, not because of secrecy of a military operation but because of a need they feel to protect the political hide of the President. If things go wrong, if it doesn't play well out there, they don't want reporters out with stories about how we actually got a note from the Grenadians saying that our safety was guaranteed as U.S. citizens but we thought we'd just go ahead with the invasion anyway. I think that's the problem here. General Vessey says secrecy, but for two days before the invasion Radio Grenada broadcast to the world that they expected it. And what are we to believe, that reporters going in with the troops would somehow have a secret radio and contact Havana? I just don't think that washes.[11]

Television also offered newspapermen a chance to get their views out before the morning edition was delivered. Howard Simons, then managing editor of *The Washington Post,* appeared on the October 26 edition of "Nightline" with the following reaction:

> It seems to me that the founding fathers invented the First Amendment to protect us against secret government. It also seems to me that every time there's been deception in this country we've paid a terrible price for it. Also, I don't know in my 30 years as a journalist of a single military operation anywhere in the world that was jeopardized by a news report. I think that what distinguishes this country from most other countries is the First Amendment, the people's right to know. And I'm outraged that there's almost a total news blackout, even to the fact that the Federal Communications Com-

mission today threatened to remove the licenses of ham radio operators who carry news reports.[12]

When challenged by Henry Catto, former Pentagon spokesman, on the relevance of the First Amendment to his "right to know" comment, Simons replied:

The phrase is not in the First Amendment, but it's in our tradition, it's in our bones, it's in our marrow. And I think . . . that all you do when you create a blackout such as this, which I say is unprecedented in peacetime, is to create the idea there's a cover-up, there's something to hide. I think the press is perfectly willing to take the risks of war as we've done since the Civil War and World War I, II, Korea, Vietnam. We're not asking for anything special in the way of protection; we can take care of ourselves. What we want to do is see for ourselves and not rely on Radio Havana and some vague reports elsewhere. I think one of the really dangerous spots in the world is Iran-Iraq, and what frightens most of us in the news business is we're not allowed to report it for the same reason.[13]

Fed only officially cleared footage and accounts, reporters became more and more intolerant of the government's reasons for press exclusion. Dan Rather, in his October 27 CBS Radio news commentary, directly criticized the military for misleading reporters and denying access to Grenada:

About the invasion of Grenada, the Defense Department today handed out its first photographs, sad, pitiful stuff, from the Army, the kind of stuff the Russians usually hand out for public consumption.

The American press wasn't allowed in, as you know. You should hear the reasons.

The other day, a general said, "We were afraid you'd get hurt." When he said this, a room full of reporters rolled their eyes toward the ceiling. They knew it wasn't true.

Then the general made a strategic retreat. He said, "The reason we didn't want the press is secrecy, the element of surprise, gentlemen." This is also untrue, the general know [sic] this and so do we.

For one thing, the night before the invasion the U.S. tipped the Soviet Union and Cuba. You know what else? Russia and Cuba were even allowed to have a ship, the *Vietnam Star,* pick up some of their people before the invasion. . . .*

---

*These two allegations remain CBS exclusives. They were denied by the State Department. The name of the Cuban ship was the *Vietnam Heroica* (see chapter 6).

The point here is that the military didn't just dummy up with the press, it didn't just mislead them. There's no joy in saying it, but they lied knowingly, deliberately. . . .

But, in this country there is a long tradition that has always overrode [sic] that antipathy, a tradition that puts the press in the battlefield so citizens at home can find out from independent reporters what's happening. But the men with stars on their shoulders who called the shots on Grenada decided, "Who cares about the press?" Which is another way of saying, "Who cares what the public knows?"[14]

Rather, in his television broadcast, also stressed more than once that the footage CBS was showing was censored by the Defense Department.[15]

Newspapers took up the cry on October 27. The *Los Angeles Times* considered the lack of information inexcusable and dangerous in its editorial "That Uncertain Feeling."[16] And the American Society of Newspaper Editors said the restrictions "go beyond the normal limits of military censorship."[17]

On the 28th, the press was still bucking futilely against restrictions. At a press conference with Larry Speakes, the feeling was clear:

Reporter: Does the White House not have any—not have any influence on this matter?

Speakes: I'm not going to debate you on it. I'm sorry . . . I'm—you—everybody here knows what we've done on that.

Reporter: You haven't done enough!

Reporter: Is it going to be the policy from now on that we get our information, not independently from—not independent sources, but only from official U.S. sources?[18]

Similar commentaries followed. *The New York Times* attacked the administration's justifications for constraints on the press as "feeble, infuriating" and rebutted each. Regarding the safety of reporters, the *Times* wrote, "Safety? Let Mr. Weinberger consider the Iwo Jima memorial, not a mile from his office—the marines raising the flag on Mount Suribachi. How much safety does he think was guaranteed to Joe Rosenthal of the Associated Press who took the famous picture?"[19]

About the need for military secrecy:

For a brief time that was a responsible concern, but to bar reporters is a sledgehammer solution . . . there's another necessity, the same one that led the Air Force to take William Laurence of the *Times* on the flight that dropped the atomic bomb on Nagasaki in 1945. Democracies depend on trust, and trust in war, small or large, depends on credible witnesses.[20]

And finally, the *Times* attacked what it called the "I'm just a civilian" justification, or the administration's deference to the military. "Mr. Weinberger's most astonishing rationale was that the commanders of the operation did not want reporters along, and he 'wouldn't ever dream of overriding a commander's decision.' What a perversion of the idea of civilian control of the military."[21]

The military allowed a pool of closely shepherded reporters to tour the Point Salines airstrip on October 27. *The Washington Post,* in its October 28 editorial, considered this too little, too late and explained:

> We say this out of more than mere pique at the theft of our journalistic function during the interval by the Pentagon, Radio Havana and the island's ham radio community. If the American media can be excluded by their own government from direct coverage of events of great importance to the American people, the whole character of the relationship between governors and governed is affected.[22]

The *St. Louis Post-Dispatch* reminded readers that "Truth is the first casualty in war,"[23] and a chorus of other editorial writers across the country joined in the criticism of the exclusion.

But there was not total consensus. A few journalists, like the *New York Post*'s, felt national security to be a valid reason for press restrictions, even on October 28, the fourth day of the invasion. " 'America First' Means Nothing to Selfish U.S. Press," a *Post* headline read, and it summoned up scenes from history exemplifying the need for secrecy during Pearl Harbor (for Japan) or the Iran rescue attempt. The *Post* concluded: "What the networks really are furious about is that they were unable to bend the U.S. government to their whims and satisfy their appetite for violent news footage."[24]

Still others, such as Reed Irvine of Accuracy in Media[25] and Jeffrey Hart in the *Colorado Springs Gazette Telegraph,*[26] suggested that journalists were biased, and the certainty of slanted antimilitary reporting was sufficient reason to exclude them from some military exercises.

But journalists for the most part were critical. Simons, managing editor of *The Washington Post,* told *Newsweek,* "If somebody had come to me and said, 'You can't report this until the operation is secure,' I would have said, 'Fine.' [But] I want to be there. I want to see it with my eyes, not the Pentagon's." The *Newsweek* article concluded, "In the end, the administration's treatment of the press in Grenada seems to reflect a larger view about freedom of information: as he has repeatedly shown, this president doesn't believe in it."[27]

The *Army Times* discussed the exclusion of press and television as an unwise act by the military in its November 14 editorial "The Secret War."[28]

Angry words were not limited to the press and television screens. On Capitol Hill, members of Congress were waging their own rhetorical battle. Senator Edward M. Kennedy (D-Mass.), member of the Armed Services Committee, delivered the following address to his colleagues:

> I am wholly unwilling to cede civilian authority on this issue. The administration's policy of censorship about events in Grenada is unprecedented, seemingly unjustified, and probably unconstitutional. . . .
>
> It is a shame that the American people learned more from ham radios and Radio Havana than from American reporters who should be in Grenada doing the job which the Constitution so properly assigns to them.[29]

On the same day, Representative Charles A. Hayes (D-Ill.) addressed the House:

> Whether or not we accept the peculiar rationale released by the administration to justify this gunboat diplomacy, the American people cannot accept, for another day, the denial of their historically hard-earned rights to have the facts of such events brought directly to them by their own free and unrestricted press. . . .
>
> The survival of our right to be informed through our own free press may well be worth whatever risks such assignments may bring to our newspeople.[30]

Many top newsmen and news executives went to Capitol Hill to attempt to loosen the administration's curb on the news. The Senate took action on October 29, when members voted 53-18 to end all restrictions on the press. Some senators, like John G. Tower (R-Tex.), thought that the action taken was too broad. "You could have reporters from Tass," he said. "Is that what you want?"[31] Other senators agreed that the resolution, which came in the form of an amendment attached to the debt ceiling bill, was "too sweeping" and should be reconsidered. Their worries were ill-founded, however, for the bill was buried amid Senate procedural red tape, and no further action was taken on the Grenada issue.

Top media figures testified before the House Judiciary Subcommittee on Courts, Civil Liberties, and the Administration of Justice on November 2. Edward Joyce, president of CBS News, expressed his fears that the strength of the First Amendment was being eroded:

> I am seriously concerned that we may indeed be witnessing the dawn of a new era of censorship, of manipulation of the press, of considering the media the handmaiden of government to spoon-feed the public with government-approved information.

If the government is permitted to abrogate the First Amendment at will, to the detriment of not simply the press but the public as well, I am concerned that such action will be taken again and again and again, whenever a government wishes to keep the public in the dark.[32]

Both John Chancellor, senior commentator, NBC News, and David Brinkley, senior correspondent, ABC News, presented views critical of the administration's curbs on press freedom, a right some soldiers on Grenada had died defending. Said Chancellor:

It is not only the privilege of the American press to be present at moments of historic importance, it is the responsibility of the press to be there. The men who died in the invasion of Grenada were representing values in American life; one of those values is the right of the citizenry to know what their government is doing. That principle, of the press as observer and as critic of the government, was established at the beginning of the United States. It is the responsibility of all citizens to uphold it.[33]

During the hearings, Representative Carlos J. Moorhead (R-Calif.) said early on-scene news coverage was banned to protect "the lives of our soldiers and sailors." Brinkley argued that the presence of reporters would not have endangered servicemen and that danger to reporters was no reason for excluding them.

There have been two basic themes in the Pentagon's resistance: The first is security of the operation; the second is the safety of the journalists who are covering it. . . . In [Indochina] we took our chances in the field with the troops and 53 newsmen were killed or are missing in the course of covering that war. An unknown number were wounded. . . .

[I]t seems to me that in a Democratic society it is essential that the people have access to information regarding the intentions and the actions of their government. This is particularly true in the case of military operations when men and women are asked to support or at least to understand a policy that may lead to the loss of their own lives or the lives of their loved ones. Last June when he retired from the Army after a distinguished career as Chief of Staff, General Edward C. Meyer said, "Soldiers should not go off to war without having the nation behind them." To which I would simply add, Amen General.[34]

Representative Moorhead stated that "informal polls" showed the public supported the government restrictions by a margin of two to one. Brinkley replied that he was surprised the margin was not closer to ten to one. "We are not leaders of a popularity contest," he said.[35]

Floyd Abrams, lawyer and First Amendment scholar, told the subcommittee that "I know of no other recent administration that has acted so consistently against the right of the public to obtain information." He added that legislative solutions were improbable; the remedy was to encourage the view that denying the public information is "un-American."[36]

But in spite of the reaction of the media, there were hints that the exclusion of the press during the first days of the Grenada operation might serve as precedent for future government policy. In November, White House chief of staff James A. Baker III told Jack Nelson of the *Los Angeles Times,* "Under similar circumstances, we would behave the same way."[37] The White House has not indicated any change from this position since then, although Larry Speakes suggested that, in his own view, total exclusion should not be repeated.[38]

The Public's Opinion

Public reaction to the limits on coverage did not echo that of the media spokesmen. A *Los Angeles Times* poll taken November 12-17 showed that 52 percent of the 2,004 adults interviewed nationwide approved of the news blackout; 41 percent disapproved. Despite this approval of press exclusion, the respondents also opposed, two to one, the idea of the blackout serving as a precedent for future war operations and believed, four to one, that journalists at the front "perform a necessary service." The *Times* also found that the more informed a respondent was on foreign affairs, the more he or she approved of media coverage and opposed censorship.[39]

The media received a harsh appraisal from Cable News Network's phone-in survey, which produced a sizable majority favoring the blackout. These and similar figures reported by newspapers and television stations across the nation caused a certain unease in the media, as evidenced by *Time* magazine's December 12 cover story, "Journalism Under Fire." *Time* explained that "the most vivid indication of the souring attitude toward the press came when the Reagan administration invaded Grenada and excluded reporters from the scene. . . . [To many] the lack of coverage seemed inconsequential—even gratifying—as if laryngitis had silenced a chronic complainer."[40]

But later looks at the figures presented a more complicated picture. The *National Journal* suggested that "despite Grenada, the public trusts the press more than the government." After Grenada, when people were asked who they thought was more truthful, "high government officials in Washington or the major news media," people trusted the news media over the government, 47-32 percent. The reason the public appeared to support the Grenada blackout, the *Journal* asserted, is because they supported the successful Grenada operation as a whole.[41]

Pollster Louis Harris took issue with the *Time* article. He conducted his own poll in early December, and the results, although partly contradictory, looked more positive for the press. Of the 1,249 polled, 65 percent believed that "a small pool of reporters should have been allowed to accompany the troops when they invaded Grenada in order to report it to the American people." Only 32 percent disagreed. Sixty-three percent believed that "by not allowing at least a small pool of reporters to report an invasion, a president or the military might be tempted to cover up mistakes or lives lost." A large majority (83 percent to 13 percent) agreed that "in a free country, such as the United States, a basic freedom is the right to know about important events, especially where the lives of American fighting men are involved." But only a bare majority (52 percent) of the respondents disagreed with the statement that "the press and TV news pry too much into too many things as it is, so it was good to put them in their place by keeping them out of Grenada." Finally, 53 percent believed that the country was "better off, not worse off, for having full and complete coverage of the Vietnam War on television and in the press."[42]

In short, the public's after-the-fact support for the press curbs in Grenada was apparently a function of approval of U.S. policy in Grenada, not an expression of overwhelming general antipathy toward the press, although nobody in the news business found cause to cheer.

Constitutional Issues

The letters of protest from the leading press organizations flowed into the White House and the Pentagon in the days following the Grenada invasion: from the Radio-Television News Directors Association (RTNDA)[43] and the American Newspaper Publishers Association (AN-PA)[44] on October 27, from the American Society of Newspaper Editors[45] (ASNE) on October 31, and from other press groups.[46] In addition, as we have noted, many newspaper, television, and radio organizations weighed in with sharply worded editorials decrying the exclusion of journalists during the first days of the operation.

Several press and civil rights groups contemplated a stronger response to what they saw as the administration's refusal to acknowledge the importance of the First Amendment.[47] "We are thinking of bringing suit as to whether there is a First Amendment right under the Constitution to be present and observe front line combat under the traditional restrictions that have been worked out since World War II," said Jack Landau, executive director of the Washington-based Reporters Committee for Freedom of the Press.[48] In mid-November, the committee retained attorney Benjamin W. Heineman, Jr., of the Washington firm Sidley & Austin, to explore the potential for legal action against the Reagan administration.

Considering a legal basis for litigation, however, was just one of the tasks facing those journalists planning a response to the media's defeat in Grenada. Forging a consensus among the diverse elements of the press and television was more problematic.

The first wild card was Larry Flynt, the publisher of *Hustler.* On October 26, the day after the invasion, Flynt filed suit in the U.S. District Court for the District of Columbia, naming as defendants Defense Secretary Caspar W. Weinberger and Secretary of State George P. Shultz. The complaint asked for an injunction and a declaratory judgment against the administration for preventing reporters employed by Larry Flynt Publications from traveling to Grenada.[49]

Many news executives shared Flynt's sentiments about the military's rebuff to journalists. But none was inclined to join him in his suit.[50] (The suit was dismissed on June 21, 1984; the appeal was scheduled to be heard in May 1985.) For one thing, Flynt's hasty move had not been coordinated with First Amendment lawyers who had long sought to expand gradually the journalist's right of access to governmental activities. The press groups were also worried about being seen by the public as supporting Flynt's peculiar views of the First Amendment, since these views had been associated with his efforts to loosen antipornography laws.[51] Floyd Abrams, a prominent First Amendment attorney who has represented *The New York Times,* voiced the general antipathy toward *Hustler*'s publisher: "Flynt is a clear and present danger to the First Amendment."[52]

Landau was more deliberate in his plans for a lawsuit. He consulted with the ad hoc planning committee of press organizations, which included representatives from the Associated Press, United Press International, and ANPA.[53] On November 30, a strategy session was held in Washington, D.C., and the outlines of a possible lawsuit were presented in the form of a brief prepared by Heineman.[54] But to Landau's apparent chagrin, the committee decided to forego legal action, opting for negotiations instead.[55]

In early December, the ad hoc committee (which now included ten press organizations, having been joined by the ASNE and the RTNDA) embarked upon a campaign to explain and restore traditional media-military relations and to win a promise from the Reagan administration that it would never again bar reporters from covering wars.[56] The committee sent two letters to President Reagan asking for a meeting with him. Although White House spokesman Peter Roussel later said the president was "aware" of the letters, neither was answered.[57]

So the committee went public, issuing a "statement of principle" on January 10, 1984.[58] The statement affirmed the need for military security and even occasional "limited" censorship. But it also called on "the highest civilian and military officers of the government" to reaffirm the "historic principle that American journalists, print and broadcast, with their professional equipment should be present" when U.S. troops go into combat. Evidence of a split in opinion about how to proceed in the face of apparent administration recalcitrance appeared in the preamble, which noted that the statement of principle was not the "position of the press" but rather the "carefully considered work of the experienced individuals" serving on the special committee.*

The statement, released to the press on January 10 and widely published the next day, apparently caught the eye of administration officials. According to several committee members, Roussel was at work arranging a meeting between the committee and administration officials within twenty-four hours of the statement's release.[59] A week later, on January 17, five press representatives, including Jerry Friedheim, executive vice president of the ANPA, and Creed Black, president of the ASNE, met with Baker, Michael Deaver, Larry Speakes, and four other White House officials.[60] Unfortunately, the president's schedule was "too crammed," Roussel said, to allow him to meet with the press delegation, as some members had hoped he would.

No decisions about press coverage of wars were made at the meeting, and participants were later circumspect in commenting on it. But Friedheim, a former Pentagon spokesman, described the meeting as "very cordial" and "useful." Some members of the press, however, were less than happy with the meeting. *Editor & Publisher* quoted one unnamed newsman who said the committee had behaved "like a bunch of frightened supplicants . . . afraid the President is going to criticize them."[61]

Another factor in the editors' and publishers' decision not to sue was an apparent effort at reconciliation launched by the Joint Chiefs of Staff in November. Chairman of the Joint Chiefs of Staff, General John W. Vessey, Jr., on November 4, 1983, announced a plan to empanel a commission (The Chairman of the Joint Chiefs of Staff Panel on Military-Media Relations) of military officers and journalists to investigate the Grenada curbs and to formulate guidelines for press coverage of future actions.[62] Vessey named a retired army major general, Winant Sidle, former military information chief in Vietnam (1967-69), to head the commission.

The proposed military hearings presented press groups with a dilemma, reflected in a background paper prepared by Jack Landau of the

---

*The member groups of this committee were the American Newspaper Publishers Association, American Society of Magazine Editors, American Society of Newspaper Editors, Associated Press Managing Editors, National Association of Broadcasters, Radio-Television News Directors Association, Reporters Committee for Freedom of the Press, Society of Professional Journalists (Sigma Delta Chi), the Associated Press, United Press International.

Reporters Committee, dated November 30. The paper mentioned the possibility of boycotting the hearings: "If there is press participation, it could be viewed as some kind of approval for the proceedings and it might allow the President, Secretary Weinberger, the Courts, and Congress to claim that the press should await the results before taking any further action before these forums." But the paper warned, "If the press stays away from the Vessey commission, the Administration will claim that the press refuses to be cooperative on this issue and will criticize any further efforts with the Administration, Courts, and Congress by stating a forum already is available to study the issue."[63]

Eventually, press groups swallowed their fear that cooperating with the Sidle commission might be taken as an indication that press access to battlefields was a negotiable issue. The ad hoc committee offered to provide witnesses to testify at the hearings, but it recommended that its members not serve on the commission itself.[64] None served.

Many media organizations, however, did respond to a questionnaire sent out by the Sidle commission on December 8, 1983, asking their opinion on, among other things, military censorship and press access.

In general, the organizations suggested that the media do have a right to access during military operations because they are the eyes of the people. None of the respondents offered a specific "kind" of access they desired; the timing, number of newspeople, and accommodations would vary, they said, according to the circumstances (e.g., whether it was a surprise attack).

They agreed that the press should be allowed maximum coverage as early as possible, but recognized that it would sometimes be impossible for reporters to accompany the first wave. "The press has an obligation to (cover military operations) within the limits of true national security and troop safety," said Keith Fuller, president·and general manager of AP.[65] "At the initiation of a military operation," said Richard Harwood, deputy managing editor of *The Washington Post,* "we want the most complete access *practicable.* "[66]

But predictable differences arose among the media groups when asked who should cover a military operation if only a two-man pool were allowed. "Tradition would suggest that they be representatives of the Associated Press and United Press International," said AP's Fuller.[67] *Newsweek* said a wire service reporter and photographer should go first but a magazine photographer should be one of the first added to an expanded pool because wire service photos (black and white) do not "fill news-magazine needs."[68] Newspapers preferred the largest pool possible.

A two-person pool is "entirely unworkable from every standpoint," asserted CNN's William Headline because television's "basic field unit" consists of a correspondent, cameraperson, technician, and producer.[69] NBC also considered a four-person crew their minimal staff.

Recognizing their own partisanship, many members of the press who objected to military restrictions did not mind the military PAOs deciding who should constitute the pools. Said Keith Fuller of AP, "Because of the natural competition among the media, a process in which the press does its own selection might not always work."[70]

Most of the respondents shied away from the issue of legal rights to access. Jerry W. Friedheim, executive vice president of the American Newspaper Publishers Association, said "The challenge for every American is to make the checks-and-balances of our constitutional system work without unnecessary litigation. Solutions acceptable to and good for all parties can be found short of the United States Supreme Court."[71] Richard Harwood of *The Washington Post* added, "We rely on historic precedent and democratic practices rather than constitutional case law (to show the rights guaranteed by the First Amendment). The First Amendment issue has not been decided and probably should not be raised through any court action."[72]

A few organizations criticized the government for asking the press to define its own rights. ANPA and ASNE, submitting similar statements, wrote: "To say, as some government spokesmen recently have, that 'this is not a matter for the government; the press must tell us what it will accept,' is, at best naive. . . . Most Administrations have planned for public information via the press."[73]

Summing up the general "press" viewpoint, Fuller of AP wrote, "Censorship is opposed as a matter of principle. To expect any other response is to fail to understand the basis on which the press is engaging in this dialogue with (the Sidle commission). . . . We would hope that [censorship] would be regarded as an extreme measure, a step to be taken only when there is in truth a clear danger to the security of the nation and the safety of the military mission. Censorship based on a will to achieve political ends will fail. And it will fail with the public as well as the press."[74]

The Sidle commission, consisting of General Sidle, six other military officers, and seven former reporters or news executives read these and other statements. They then questioned nineteen representatives of major newspapers, magazines, wire services, television networks, and professional associations, as well as three representatives from the military public affairs and information offices from February 6-10. With this information, they drew up a report recommending a course of action for the military and the media.

After a review by Pentagon Chief Spokesman Michael I. Burch and Secretary of Defense Caspar W. Weinberger, the Sidle commission report was released on August 23, 1984. It walked the line between the military and the media, stating it was "consistent" with both Weinberger's vague post-Grenada "Principles of Information" (released December 1, 1983) and part of the ad hoc journalists' committee's "Statement of Principle on Press Access to Military Operations."

The report offered eight recommendations: public affairs planning should be made concurrently with the operational planning; if a media pool is the only way to provide media access to a military operation, the pool should be the largest possible and maintained only as long as necessary; the secretary of defense should consider and decide whether to prepare a ready list of accredited reporters to use in case a pool is required; media access should depend on the media's voluntary compliance with security guidelines; public affairs planning should include sufficient equipment and personnel to assist correspondents; planners should strive to accommodate journalists at the earliest time possible without interfering with combat operations; planners should attempt to include "intra- and inter-theater transportation" for media personnel; and finally, the members of military public affairs and news organizations should meet to discuss their differences. The panel also suggested that the secretary of defense meet with representatives from the broadcast media to discuss the problems with press access versus military security.[75]

Preceding this set of recommendations was a letter from General Sidle to General Vessey. "You did not request our assessment of media handling of Grenada and we will not provide it," wrote Sidle. He then added: "However, we do feel that had our recommendations been 'in place' and fully considered at the time of Grenada, there might have been no need to create our panel."[76]

Weinberger's official response to the Sidle report consisted mainly of a news release, which his office attached to the report. Aside from commending the members of the panel and reiterating the need for better military-media relations, Weinberger assigned Assistant Secretary of Defense (Public Affairs) Michael Burch to "take the necessary steps" to implement the recommendations of the Sidle commission for maximum news coverage of military operations balanced with the need for military security.[77]

On October 3, 1984, Burch met with representatives of both the print and broadcast media. The initial outcome was the recommendation to form a press pool of eleven people (one reporter from both AP and UPI, one newsperson each from ABC, CBS, NBC, and CNN, a camera operator and a sound technician to be shared by the four networks, a photographer, a radio broadcaster, and a magazine writer). No representative from any daily newspaper was included. The immediate uproar from both newspaper and television representatives (the latter group included Edward Joyce, president of CBS News) produced a revised pool plan the next day which included a reporter from a daily newspaper.

Burch stated that the secretary of defense "can dictate a national policy on how an operation is covered." The news pool, he added, "will be more or less selected by us. . . . There will be some consultation, but the final decisions are ours."[78]

*   *   *

Although most press groups seemed content with a nonconfrontational approach, Landau did not immediately abandon thoughts of a lawsuit. Shortly after the November 30 agreement among press groups to pursue negotiations in lieu of litigation, Landau published a call-to-arms in *Editor & Publisher,* chiding the publishers for their timidity. Landau argued that, in previous First Amendment cases that the press ultimately lost, editors and publishers "were willing to take the risk because the principle of public information was so important and the danger to the public would be so great without some type of challenge being mounted." He argued that the Grenada exclusion case was stronger than other cases the press had litigated. "Why then," Landau asked, "are many of the media lawyers telling their news organizations that the risk should not be taken?"[79]

The Reporters Committee, with Heineman's counsel, had initially considered a number of possible legal principles on which a lawsuit might be based. These were spelled out in Landau's November 30 background paper.[80]

Denial of Equal Protection. By preventing American reporters from covering the invasion while allowing three members of the foreign press and a number of American civilians to roam freely on Grenada, the U.S. military may have engaged in a denial of "equal protection" under the Fourteenth Amendment, the Reporters Committee found.[81] The evidence indicates that American reporters were singled out for deception by the government. According to the background paper, the governments of Cuba and the Soviet Union, as well as West European allies, were notified "five hours" prior to the start of the invasion, effectively giving advance notice to foreign press organizations and enabling them to send reporters to the island.[82] (The State Department on October 26 said the Soviets and Cubans had been advised as the invasion began.) Meanwhile, American reporters were relegated to the sidelines. Furthermore, only members of the private press were discriminated against. Military reporters and camera teams were mustered a day and a half in advance so that they could be moved to Grenada as quickly as possible.[83]

Prior Restraint. The military authorities "arrested" four reporters (the Ed Cody affair) and held them "incommunicado on a naval vessel for three days." This act the background paper termed a "prior restraint by false imprisonment." And when Vice Admiral Joseph Metcalf "threatened to destroy privately chartered vehicles used by [the] American press attempting to reach the island," he perpetrated a "prior restraint by death threats." The paper noted that the Supreme Court has frequently affirmed its aversion to such prepublication restraints on freedom of the press.[84]

Dissemination of Misleading Information. Under federal criminal laws, government officials are prohibited from intentionally disseminating false and misleading information. This law was used to good effect in the 1977 federal prosecution of former Maryland Governor Marvin Mandel, according to the background paper.[85] Examples of the administration's deception included "self-serving" changes in the estimate of the number of Cubans on the island, and a failure to inform the public about the bombing of a mental hospital in St. George's until four days after the fact.[86] By preventing reporters from verifying these claims, the government may have illegally induced the press to expend money to publish false statements, the background paper said.

These three possible causes of action were outlined in the background paper, but the strongest basis for a suit was found in a line of First Amendment cases granting the press a "right of access." The Reporters Committee noted that "Supreme Court and other cases guarantee . . . First Amendment right of access by the press to report significant government actions, particularly government actions to which the press has *historically* and *traditionally* had access" (emphasis theirs). To facilitate the press's efforts to report on such "government actions," the courts have granted reporters access to White House sidewalks and press facilities, wartime military bases, town meetings, and courtrooms, the background paper contends.[87]

The leading Supreme Court pronouncement on the media's right of access appears in *Richmond Newspapers Inc. v. Virginia,* a 1982 case in which the Court, by a 7-1 vote, overturned a trial judge's decision to exclude reporters from a criminal trial.[88] Chief Justice Warren Burger found that in the Anglo-American legal system, the criminal trial, "throughout its evolution . . . has been open to all who care to observe."[89] This tradition of openness was declared by the Court to be embedded in the Constitution.

"The First Amendment goes beyond protection of the press and the self-expression of individuals to prohibit government from limiting the stock of information from which members of the public may draw," Burger wrote.[90] In a concurring opinion, Justice John Paul Stevens commented on the significance of the decision: "Today. . . for the first time, the Court unequivocally holds that an arbitrary interference with access to important information is an abridgment of the freedoms of speech and of the press protected by the First Amendment."[91]

The Court extended the protection of the First Amendment beyond news-disseminating to news-gathering because of the vital importance of the latter function in a democracy, the Court said. "People in an open society do not demand infallibility from their institutions, but it is difficult for them to accept what they are prohibited from observing."[92] Popular control of government requires that independent observers be allowed to monitor the operations of government, the Court added. If such freedom to observe is withdrawn, "important aspects of freedom of speech and 'of the press could be eviscerated.' "[93]

The Historical Record

With *Richmond Newspapers* in mind, the Reporters Committee conducted a survey of press coverage of "all [U.S.] military engagements from 1754-1983 including twenty-two Caribbean expeditions from 1880-1922." The findings convinced the committee that wars, like criminal trials, have traditionally been open to observers, and therefore cannot constitutionally be closed to the press.[94]

A December 5 draft of a White Paper prepared by the Reporters Committee distinguished between covert actions, such as the Iranian hostage rescue attempt, and overt military operations, which involve large numbers of troops for possibly extended periods of time and which are expected to be observed by large numbers of people. The press, which has never demanded access to covert operations, has always managed to reach "sensitive and sensible accommodations" with the national security concerns of the executive branch, the paper said. Even if a military action is overt, the paper conceded that "the presence of the media with the troops may nonetheless be conditioned by limits on the number of journalists and on the content or timing of dispatches."[95]

In Grenada, however, reporters were not just regulated, they were completely excluded. By violating the traditional openness of U.S. military actions, the Reagan administration had trampled on the First Amendment, the White Paper concluded.

Commenting on the prognosis for a lawsuit based on the exclusion of reporters from Grenada, Floyd Abrams remarked at a November 1983 Practicing Law Institute seminar on communications: "The legal claim to have some press present at front line combat areas such as in Grenada is probably a stronger constitutional claim than the claim for press access to trials." Abrams added, however, that the Supreme Court would probably rule against the press anyway.[96]

Even on its merits, the case would not have been a sure thing. *Richmond Newspapers* contains a potential stumbling block in the way of a successful First Amendment suit against the Department of Defense for barring reporters from a battlefield, a weakness that the Reporters Committee attempted to gloss over. In the committee's background paper and in an article by Landau in *Editor & Publisher,* a passage from the opinion was quoted to the effect that "The right of access to places traditionally open . . . may be seen as assured . . . by the First Amendment guarantees of speech and press."[97] The first ellipsis, however, clipped off three important words. The full quote reads: "The right of access to places traditionally open *to the public,* as criminal trials have long been, may be seen as assured by the amalgam of the First Amendment guarantees of speech and press [emphasis added]."[98]

If the historical record were to reveal that U.S. troops on the battlefields have not traditionally been open to the "public," then the Supreme Court might balk at applying the principles of *Richmond Newspapers* to the events in Grenada. Indeed, in places where the public has not generally had a right of access, the Supreme Court has often barred reporters. In a 1974 case, *Saxbe v. The Washington Post Co.,* the Court upheld by a 5-4 margin a prison regulation limiting reporters' access to inmates.[99] "The Constitution does not . . . require government to accord the press special access to information not shared by members of the public generally," the Court concluded.[100] A footnote gave the rationale for drawing such a limit on news-gatherers' freedom of movement:

> There are few restrictions on action which could not be clothed by ingenious argument in the garb of decreased data flow. For example, the prohibition of unauthorized entry into the White House diminishes the citizen's opportunities to gather information he might find relevant to his opinion of the way the country is being run, but that does not make entry into the White House a First Amendment right. The right to speak and publish does not carry with it the unrestrained right to gather information.[101]

The extent of press access to government activities was also limited by *Gannett Co. v. DePasquale,* a 1979 case in which the Court held that a pretrial hearing on a motion to suppress prejudicial evidence could be closed to the press. The Court appeared to base its ruling on the temporary nature of the restriction and on the fact that after the danger of prejudice had passed a transcript of the hearing would be released, fulfilling the public's need to know.[102]

In *Richmond Newspapers,* Chief Justice Burger emphasized that the *Gannett* ruling pertained only to pretrial hearings, not trials. But just how *Gannett* distinguished pretrial hearings from trials has never been clear. (Because pretrial hearings have not traditionally been open to the public? Because the public can be informed about the hearings by means other than the attendance of reporters?) The confusion over the interpretation of the case was noted in Justice Harry Blackmun's concurring opinion in *Richmond Newspapers,* which cited law review commentaries titled, "*Gannett* Means What It Says; But Who Knows What It Says?" and "The Boner Called *Gannett.*"[103]

Whatever it means, *Gannett* does not encourage lawyers for press groups to seek to extend their right of access.

*   *   *

The parameters of the press's legal right of access, as created by the Supreme Court to date, are themselves uncertain and therefore not inviolable. The First Amendment sometimes runs up against countervailing sections of the Constitution, most notably Article II, which grants the president, as chief executive and commander-in-chief, authority over foreign and military affairs.[104]

In adjudicating such conflicts between freedom of the press and national security, the Supreme Court has used an ad hoc balancing approach, weighing the strength of the competing claims.[105] Article II has frequently proven to be the more compelling of the two sections of the Constitution. For example, the right of the government to bar travel to Communist Cuba was upheld in *Zemel v. Rusk* (1965), even though this restriction might limit the ability of American citizens (including journalists) to gather information.[106]

In other contexts as well, the exceptionally broad authority of the president over the conduct of foreign (as opposed to domestic) affairs has been repeatedly affirmed since the landmark 1936 case, *United States of America v. Curtiss-Wright Export Corp.,* which upheld the power of the president to restrict arms exports.[107]

First Amendment interests have also occasionally outweighed the president's Article II powers. In *New York Times v. United States* (the 1971 Pentagon Papers case), for example, Justice Hugo L. Black noted that the Bill of Rights was appended to the Constitution two years after the latter had been written, for the express purpose of restricting the general powers granted to the executive, judicial, and legislative branches.[108]

The *Times* had challenged the government's "prior restraint" on publication of secret military *historical* documents; the case did *not* involve a ruling on the newspaper's right of access. Nonetheless, the fact that the Court held, by a vote of 6-3, that the rights of the press outweighed the alleged threat to national security is pertinent to other First Amendment disputes.

As one of the six who favored the rights of the press, Justice Black stated in his concurring opinion:

> The press was protected so that it could bare the secrets of government and inform the people. Only a free and unrestrained press can effectively ex-

pose deception in government. And paramount among the responsibilities of a free press is the duty to prevent any part of the government from deceiving the people and sending them off to distant lands to die of foreign fevers and foreign shot and shell.[109]

Discerning which way the Supreme Court might swing in balancing the First Amendment rights of the press to cover the invasion of Grenada against the Reagan administration's prerogatives to conduct a military assault as it sees fit was the main tactical question confronting the news media. The consensus among prominent First Amendment attorneys was not favorable. Robert Sack, who represents *The Wall Street Journal,* E. Barrett Prettyman, Abrams, and Heineman agreed that the Court would probably rule in favor of Article II.[110]

Aside from the weaknesses in the merits of the case, Prettyman mentioned "practical and quasi-political" difficulties. "The Supreme Court as it is presently constituted is simply not going to hold that the President must take reporters with him wherever he's going," he said.[111] Losing a lawsuit over Grenada would not only serve as a legal setback in the favorably evolving line of press access cases. A loss would also serve as a public rebuke to the Fourth Estate, whose growing claims to special treatment were viewed with mixed feelings by the public at large, judging by the polls.

Most press organizations and individual newspapers seemed to have been deterred from going forward with a lawsuit by the legal uncertainties and the inauspicious political atmosphere, Landau observed. "It [political reality] wasn't a factor with us [the Reporters Committee]. But it certainly was with the publishers and the editors. They thought that the president's action was highly popular and that a suit would be seen as an attack on the president himself, an attack on the invasion."[112]

As of early spring 1985, no court tests seemed in view. The implementation of the Sidle panel's recommendations—at least in part—were being discussed quietly between the Pentagon public affairs officers and representatives of leading news organizations. Most of the negotiations centered on the formation, exercise, and functioning of the prearranged "press pool" for hastily mounted military operations. These were largely operational issues. Defense Secretary Weinberger was invited to speak to the April convention in Washington of the American Society of Newspaper Editors. He did so, dealing primarily with the defense budget and military policy. He did not discuss the issue which had so aroused editors and televison newsfolk only eighteen months earlier. Nor did the editors ask him any questions about his view of government-media relations—to the surprise of his staff.

Yet, the post-Grenada atmosphere remains unhealthy. There are irritations—normal irritations—on both sides. But the Reagan administration has let its irritation show—in part by public complaints not only over publication of individual stories that it deems inimical to the national interest but also against what Secretary of State Shultz calls the lowering of standards by all journalists. And editorial response has been predictable. There has been no broad policy statement by either the White House or Defense Secretary Weinberger reaffirming the importance of traditional press coverage of U.S. military operations overseas. The antagonisms bared by Grenada have yet to dissipate.

· 8 ·

TWO CULTURES

THE unusual lack of access *imposed* by the Reagan administration on the press and television during the first days of Grenada was explained publicly—and somewhat imprecisely—as due to considerations of safety, logistics, or surprise by Defense Secretary Caspar Weinberger and other spokesmen in Washington. But, as we have seen, the constraints—sought by the Joint Chiefs of Staff and approved by the White House—also reflected a widespread post-Vietnam suspicion of the news media among both military and civilian officials. They feared that the media, especially television, which had replaced print as the chief object of distrust, would adopt an automatic bias against the operation, highlighting the inevitable losses and difficulties, fueling criticism back home, and, in effect, as Vice Admiral Joseph Metcalf noted, forcing the field commanders to think about public relations instead of military operations.

Secretary of State George Shultz, a former marine, expressed this sentiment rather clearly: "These days, in the adversary journalism that's been developed, it seems as though the reporters are always against us. And when you are trying to conduct a military operation, you don't need that."[1] John E. Murray, retired army major general and old Vietnam hand, observed in *The Wall Street Journal* that "Engaging the press while engaging the enemy is taking on one adversary too many. It's easier to straighten out an erratic [military maneuver] than straightening out the misconceptions of the media."[2]

The recent history of wartime military-press relations, even during World War II, makes it all too clear that there is a built-in "cultural" conflict between the military and the media, to say nothing of their workaday needs. That gap may now be widening.

The World of the Soldier

The military ideals center on the words "duty, honor, country." The military leader, as Morris Janowitz has observed, is "an officer and a gentleman." He is a member of a hierarchy, with a clear order of

133

rank and with a defined career ladder. He must, of necessity, be a team player, who may disagree with his superiors but, after offering his arguments, must carry out their orders.[3] If he finds advancement blocked or his superiors unbearable, he cannot easily change jobs; he may have to leave the service. Particularly in peacetime, in order to succeed, he must avoid embarrassment: he must deal with both routine and a myriad of "people problems," red tape, and petty detail. If he is a unit commander, he must learn how to motivate and lead ordinary men, using as his prime tools unit pride and cohesion.

In wartime, the commander faces the real test. He must exhibit confidence, know the capabilities of his men and their equipment, act decisively on insufficient information, carry out the mission, and in part, trust to luck—and he must do all of this in the organized chaos of battle. In the current American context, he must prevail over the foe while losing as few men as possible, and killing as few civilians as possible. Failure means not only personal disgrace but the futile deaths of his men and possibly the defeat of his country.[4]

The great majority of officers, of course, do not face the real test: They are technicians, staff officers, managers of the vast support system that modern warfare now requires. In some ways, their peacetime tasks are indistinguishable from those of civilians in business or government. The senior commanders do not come from these ranks; they tend to be "conservative"—in the sense that they set great store by tradition and the "old virtues"[5]—and they ultimately set the tone for all.

By British or German standards, the American military culture is highly informal, especially in the air force and army. These services, in peacetime, tend to reflect, to a considerable degree, the manners and mores of the larger society. In a real sense, the military since World War II has served as a vanguard of social change, notably with respect to racial integration. (Not surprisingly, the partial integration of women has proved, in many ways, far more difficult.) Discipline is less than harsh. Even so, the bottom line remains and is constantly invoked: duty, honor, country.[6]

As in the past, few military commanders are zealots on economic matters, except as they worry about the radical ups and downs (reflecting national moods) in defense spending.[7] They obey their civilian superiors, although with some resentment over the politicians' chronic quest for short-term political gain. After long experience with men in uniform, they take a skeptical view of the practicality of generalized social uplift. Now, as in the past, they worry about the public's readiness to sacrifice for the nation, the stress on consumerism, self-interest, hedonism—on "rights" as opposed to "duties." Not surprisingly, given the media's focus on conflict, deviance, and melodrama, most senior military men do not see the media as allies of civic peace and virtue.

The senior military officers are no longer primarily drawn, as they were prior to World War II, from the southern gentry or the northern upper-middle class. The typical officers' club smacks more of the Holiday Inn than of the Chevy Chase Club, and the sheer size of the officer corps makes it unlikely that the small, self-contained service community that prevailed prior to World War II will reemerge.

Robert Lichter and Stanley Rothman, whose work on media elites and business elites has already been cited, have surveyed attitudes, social origins, and voting habits of the "military elite."[8] In general, they find no less a gap between senior military officers and those in the media than between businessmen and journalists, but on some topics businessmen and the military do not see eye to eye either (a finding that reaffirms the conclusions of Janowitz thirty years ago). In general, the military remain "conservative" on social values, responsive to political candidates who favor higher defense spending, and far less apt than media people to see the United States and the West as the source of the Third World's problems. According to Lichter and Rothman, their social values are closer to those of Middle America than to those of the more permissive members of the media on such matters as adultery, homosexuality, and abortion.[9]

The senior officers are from Middle America mostly, and academy graduates aside, they did not attend elite colleges.[10] On the other hand, they keep going to school. The army, in particular, encourages graduate education; peacetime service abroad brings a certain worldly sophistication; the senior generals and admirals are no strangers to political Washington or to diplomatic life.

In peacetime, the senior military officers are, in fact, deeply involved in bureaucratic politics. Troops and equipment must be kept in as high a state of readiness as possible despite the distractions of peacetime. But in Washington, each service chief is preoccupied with maintaining or enlarging "budget share," devising strategic rationales for his service's claims, and adjudicating competing intraservice claims for budget priority (e.g., aircraft carriers versus nuclear submarines in the navy). He and his staff, therefore, must pay heed to the mood of Congress, the predilections of the White House and the secretary of defense, and stories in the press and television that may affect the service's image. Not surprisingly, the "negative" stories (of scandal, misdeeds, mismanagement, "waste") not only loom largest in the minds of Washington newsmen (they are more exciting to read) but also in the memories of the senior military (accurate or not, such stories may damage a man's career); such stories may be exploited by rival services or by critics of the military on Capitol Hill, and they always tend to cause distress within the Pentagon.

The Journalists' Working Life

The news media, like the armed services, have their various branches—wire services, newspapers, news magazines, radio, television—each with its own incentives and practices. Journalists also have developed a public theology: the press seeks out the facts, acts as "watchdog" over government, provides the truth so that serious citizens may decide; it may even serve as a kind of fourth branch of government.[11] The First Amendment assures journalists of the right to publish—and is interpreted by some journalists as encompassing the right to gather news. But there is no counterpart in journalism to "duty, honor, country," or to the military leader's ultimate responsibility for life and death and the nation's security.

In peacetime, a free and vigorous press keeps democracy vigorous. Yet, as the military will point out, a democracy in wartime can survive without a First Amendment (indeed, press freedom is usually curbed), but it cannot survive without a successful military defense.

During the cold war, the ambiguities of "national security" have led to recurrent debate over the press's rights and responsibilities—a debate that intensified during the Vietnam conflict, when White House credibility was at an unusually and increasingly low ebb.

Coexisting with journalism's public theology is an underlying reality: the news organizations are relatively small, competing *commercial* enterprises, operating under economic constraints, heavily dependent on attracting and retaining sufficiently large audiences to draw advertising and thus revenue. If reporters often "write for each other," their superiors have the audience in mind; and they shape the "news" at least in part with an eye toward the average reader's or viewer's presumed interests or tastes.

Producing a network evening news show (or even a small segment of it) requires a high degree of coordination, supervision, editing skill, processing, and sizable numbers of support personnel. As NBC's Douglas Kiker once said, television newsmen are engaged in "making little movies."[12] News magazine stories are products of group journalism: field reporters, often dispersed; researchers; rewritemen; editors. Wire services, through the editing and rewriting process, may blend the work of several field reporters. Newspapers, however, rely most heavily on the individual reporter in the field; his story may be shortened or dropped entirely but, under the rules of the craft, it is seldom totally rewritten. It is the newspaper, oldest of the media, that provides the essentials of journalism's public theology, and it is here that the watchdog function is most highly rewarded in terms of professional esteem.

It is often said by newspapermen that they provide the first rough draft of history. But it is a very rough draft, for journalists are not political scientists or military analysts, intelligence officers or foreign policy historians. News is not simply information. *The Washington Post* is not the *World Almanac* (or even, say, the *Congressional Quarterly*). Newsmen are both fact-gatherers and *storytellers*—their product is not called a "report" or a "study." It is called a "story." And much "news" consists simply of good "stories," dramas with human appeal. Every news organization's idea of a good story is just a little bit different. Warehouse fires, airplane crashes, murder trials, train wrecks, are always good "stories": they are diverting incidents. News, depending on the standards of the producing organization, is in part an art form. The conventions are learned on the job.

As Roger Rosenblatt pointed out in *Time*:

> Journalism tends to focus on the poor [for example] when the poor make news, usually dramatic news like a tenement fire or a march on Washington. But the poor are poor all the time. It is not journalism's ordinary business to deal with the unstartling normalities of life. Reporters need a *story*, something shapely and elegant. Poverty is disorderly, anticlimactic and endless. . . .
>
> Journalism inevitably imposes forms of order on both the facts in a story and on the arrangement of stories itself. The structures of magazines and newspapers impose one kind of order, radio and television another, usually sequential. But every form journalism takes is designed to draw the public's attention to what the editors deem most important in a day's or week's events. This naturally violates the larger truth of a chaotic universe.[13]

What kind of people are journalists? Like military life, the life of the journalist appeals to certain personality types. But recruits to journalism are usually very different from those who join the military. Journalists, however pressed by deadlines, by the tastes of superiors, by constraints of space and time, by the search for fresh information, are not *doers*, but observers. Reporters have no rank. Their status depends in large measure on their affiliation with (and within) a news organization ("I'm Joe Smith of *The New York Times*"). They have little or no responsibility for other people. They are not team players, but competitive types within their own organizations, determined to keep up with, or beat, other news organizations. They are aggressive—on occasion, they must, by telephone or in person, cajole reluctant people into divulging information. They must necessarily both confront and gain the confidence of people in authority. They are "watchdogs," but in Washington by far the largest share of their work consists of transmitting "official" news (of the executive branch or of Congress), based on official sources and, when possible, giving "both sides of the story."

These reporters and their bosses must deal with a variety of ever-changing "realities"; in order to retain sanity, they must reduce com-

plexity to a changing set of cliches. They have little time, or tempera-
ment, for reflection on the "national interest" or the Big Picture; they
must operate on professional instincts; their memories are overwhelmed
by the daily rush of new experiences, new faces, new facts—indeed,
they prize novelty. As storytellers, they prefer stories of "people" to stories
of organizations, they prefer politics to government; they prefer "action"
or "events" to "patterns" or "trends." They like to be "in the know";
they are quickly bored or frustrated when there is no "news," no new
"turn" of events. Yet they hate to be taken unawares. Big surprises are
unpleasant. They may require a journalist to assimilate a new set of
"facts" instantly and then to explain them under a tight deadline, which
often means discarding acquired wisdom; it is no wonder that journalists
tend to overreact, like Wall Street, to surprise, and tend to magnify any
sudden crisis.

Almost as if in compensation for these professional strains, reporters
are permitted a certain latitude in dress, behavior, off-duty life. The
cynical, hard-drinking reporter of *The Front Page* may have yielded to
the well-paid liberal arts graduate who writes "news analysis" as well
as "straight news." But a certain tolerance and rumpled informality still
characterize the craft. Getting an important fact wrong, by omission or
commission, prompts more frowns from the editors than it once did,
but, unless libel is involved, it seldom leads to dismissal. Of late, errors may lead to published corrections. Editors do not like to discourage
reporters unduly from the pursuit of good stories. On most newspapers,
the reporter who does not *produce* many good page-one stories is in
more trouble than the reporter who produces such stories that may, occasionally, be a bit one-sided, unduly alarmist, or "biased."

The radical newcomer is, of course, television news, whose demands
on correspondents are far more exacting. Television news is the offspring
of Hollywood, the newsreels, and radio broadcasting; as ABC Producer
Av Westin once put it, television news is just another branch of television.[14] It is a different art form, only thinly related to print. If the print
media have a fondness for the emotive "human interest" story as a side
dish to the "hard news," television lives by it. No print journalist on
a major newspaper or wire service would be permitted the latitude allowed
television reporters as they interpret on-camera the carefully edited film
snippets that appear on the network evening news shows. Indeed, the
vignette, often presented by the correspondent as a "microcosm" of the
larger event, is the goal of television news. The important thing for the
television correspondent is to be there with his camera crew—at the
firefight, at the warehouse fire, at the protest demonstration, at the
spectacle—and get a filmed bit of drama with his brief narration to New
York in time for the evening news. Unlike the print journalist, the television reporter cannot recoup. Either his cameraman has "good film" or

he does not. To the television reporter, the fact-gathering, the map-briefings, and "information" are secondary; in a fifty-word script, he cannot use much information anyway; and what the home office wants him to do, essentially, is direct the making of a vivid little action film, and supply theme and coherence to the pictures with his script.

As Michael Arlen noted, what is important is not just the reality of the filmed event, but what the audience can be made to *feel* about it.[15]

The reporter works for a television network whose existence is mapped by audience ratings; his superiors are well-paid but suffer from chronic turnover; like an actor, he has an agent to represent him in negotiations with his employer. He is a "name," a face. His world is vastly different from that of his faceless print colleagues.

The Journalists' World View

Are journalists' biases political? Much has been written since Vietnam and Watergate about "bias" in the news. And there is no question that, when they step into the voting booths, journalists tend to vote Democratic. Lichter and Rothman interviewed 240 journalists and broadcasters working for the big-league news media. They did not separate the differences in views of reporters and supervisors, those in broadcast or print news. But their findings would at first glance suggest that the charges of "liberal bias" were well-founded. For example, during the four presidential elections from 1964 to 1976, an average of 86 percent of their respondents voted for the Democratic candidate. On some issues, notably abortion, affirmative action, environmental protection, they strongly favored the liberal side. Fifty-four percent of them described themselves as "liberals" or "left of center," while only 19 percent described themselves as "conservatives."[16]

Yet, as other analysts point out, one must examine more closely how deeply held these personal views are, and how important they are in the selection and treatment of news stories on given topics. For example, in a widely quoted interview with *Variety*, Walter Cronkite defined himself as a liberal, and defined liberal as "one who is not bound by doctrine or committed to a point of view in advance."[17]

Herbert J. Gans said that the liberalism of journalists is a synonym for being "independent, open-minded, or both."[18] Michael Robinson suggests that the television networks in particular seem to be, in the final product, "cynical, yes, but liberal, no . . . over the long haul, the national press is biased against everybody [in authority] but in near equal proportions."[19]

Both Gans and Austin Ranney suggest that for television, in particular, the ideological bias is not partisan, in the sense of being Republican or Democrat. It is a legacy of the Progressive movement at the turn of the century, when muckraking journalists like Lincoln Steffans maintained that the journalist's prime purpose was to uncover the wrongdoing and chicanery of big-city politicians, the robber barons, and other villains in positions of power. Such exposure of abuses would encourage serious citizens to band together to throw out the rascals, to change things, to put enlightened reformers in office. This spirit fits in with journalism's theology. Indeed, newspapermen have always cherished exposes of individual official wrongdoing, particularly those which prompt remedial or punitive action by prosecutors or legislative committees. Such exposes are "good stories." They get Pulitzer Prizes. They satisfy journalism's claim under the First Amendment to social utility beyond the simple transmission of news or distractions.

From progressivism comes the self-image of the press as the watchdog of all in authority, military or political. It is a self-image that may wax, as during the Watergate era, and wane, as it has of late. But it leads to "good" stories, particularly television stories, of individuals against authority (enlisted men against the brass), of dissident movements, of victims of war, corporate greed or poverty—stories which have intrinsic appeal. In matters of crime, for example, the press likes "crime waves" (real or imagined), but through the neo-Progressive 1970s, the plight of convicted murderers, rapists, and muggers locked up in prisons ("prison reform") got far more attention than the plight of their victims. This was not simply a question of populism; it was also the fact that investigating reporters could see the prisons, the "system," and the unhappy prisoners as an all-of-a-piece story; they could not see the victims in a single dramatic setting.

But overall, the biases of the press, and particularly television, are professional biases; for example, the incident that, by implication at least, can be presented as a "microcosm," a "symbolic" story (e.g., the Zippo-burning of Cam Ne hamlet in Vietnam) or exposed as a "cover-up" (e.g., the Pentagon's failure to announce the bombing of the [unmarked] mental hospital on Grenada). They like "people" stories rather than complicated "policy" or "organization" stories. They are easily bored.

The anti-authority biases do not manifest themselves in an all-pervasive manner. Journalists are dependent on their news sources, whether presidents or generals, and the president gets his say. Most news is "official news." But if any authority figure is found consistently to contradict himself, manipulate the facts, shave the truth, the journalists will dutifully report what he (or she) has said; but they will begin to grumble among themselves, to nitpick his statements, and to listen to his critics, and, when Big Bad Events catch him, they will not give him the benefit of the doubt.

Such was the fate of Lyndon Johnson at Tet in 1968 and Richard Nixon in 1973-74, and, to this day, there are military men (and others) who blame it all on the media's liberal bias.

They cannot explain the success of Ronald Reagan, who, according to his aide, Michael Deaver, has "enjoyed a fair press,"[20] despite the lack of ideological sympathy among White House reporters. Why is this? The populism of the news media is selective. Newsmen respond to officials who are not afraid of them. Most of all, they respect winners (and pick on losers). They respond to candor, friendliness, and coherence, and distrust excessive "salesmanship."

General Creighton W. Abrams enjoyed a generally favorable press during his difficult 1968-73 tour as U.S. commander in Vietnam. He regarded the press as a necessary evil. He did not attempt to "sell" administration policy. He sent newsmen with his troops into Cambodia in 1970. He met with individual senior newsmen in Saigon but otherwise kept a low profile. As noted earlier, he held no press conferences, unlike his predecessor General William C. Westmoreland, who, deferring to Lyndon Johnson's wishes, twice came home to Washington to shore up public support for a war policy with which, on major strategic issues, he privately disagreed. In media retrospectives on the war, Westmoreland has suffered for that high visibility ever since.

When Two Cultures Meet

The military culture, with its accent on conformity, control, discipline, accountability, group loyalty, and cohesion, finds itself in wartime up against a group that is individualistic, competitive, word-conscious, impatient, lacking internal "rules" or "standards," varied in its needs, suspicious of authority, and hard-pressed by deadlines and the need to obtain good film or definitive information on short notice to satisfy the home office.

However, as experiences in Vietnam, Korea, and World War II made clear, the two cultures can work together when the military sets out consistent ground rules and is able to enforce them impartially and with some intelligence. In many ways, besides the lack of censorship, the Vietnam experience, which now looms large in memory, was an aberration: the abundance of logistical, transport, and communications support; the size and wide deployment of U.S. forces; and the low intensity of the ground war made it possible for U.S. field commanders to accommodate sizable numbers of print and television journalists even during the 1968 Tet offensive. The very nature of the American war—with few tactical moves by division-sized units but lots of quick moves by smaller U.S. units—made secrecy less important than in Korea or World War II: Hanoi may have had excellent local intelligence, but it did not or could not exploit it in a sustained battle.

Both technology and the way U.S. forces are expected to deploy in any future limited wars should provoke some second thoughts on military-press relations. Grenada may be a better model for future U.S. intervention than was the slow buildup in Vietnam or the shift of U.S. forces across the straits between Japan and South Korea in 1950.

In any operations in the Third World, by all accounts U.S. forces will be hastily deployed; the availability of bases is problematic; there is unlikely to be the equivalent of a Saigon, a Seoul, a Tokyo, or a London as a comfortable rear camp for journalists. Even Grenada may look like an easy-access story, in retrospect, to journalists who attempt to cover widely dispersed U.S. marine, airborne, and naval units along the shores of the Persian Gulf. The very austerity and dispersion of American forces in such operations may make secrecy, deception, and surprise (hence press censorship) an integral part of U.S. tactics, as was the case for the British in the Falklands. In Central America, closer to home, any U.S. military operations might be less austere, and constraints on journalists less forbidding. But it is difficult to imagine that the military's large and slow buildup, easy stance on security, and abundant accommodations for newspeople in Vietnam will be repeated when journalists accompany U.S. forces on limited wars in the future. The members of the two cultures have some major adjustments to make.

NOTES

Chapter 1

1. Transcript from "Nightline," ABC-TV, October 26, 1983, p. 10.
2. Edward Nichols, "Behind the Grenada Media War," *San Diego Union,* November 6, 1983, p. C1.
3. John Chancellor commentary, NBC News, October 26, 1983.
4. Jack Nelson, "Bare Majority Backs Grenada News Blackout," *Los Angeles Times,* November 20, 1983, p. 1.
5. Jeremiah O'Leary, "Raiding and Writing Don't Mix, Shultz Says," *Washington Times,* December 16, 1983, p. 1.
6. John E. Murray, "Journalists in the Press of Battle," letter to the editor, *Wall Street Journal,* November 4, 1983.
7. "Metcalf Says Military People Have a Dislike for the Press," *Navy Times,* advance release, January 16, 1984.
8. Roone Arledge, statement submitted to the Chairman of the Joint Chiefs of Staff's Media and Military Relations Panel (the Sidle Committee), January 30, 1984. Arledge is the president of ABC News.
9. Jack Foisie, "Press-Military Relations," *Nieman Reports* (Spring 1984), pp. 15-16.
10. William W. Headline, statement submitted to the Sidle Committee, January 27, 1984. Headline is the bureau chief of Cable News Network.
11. Edward O. Fritts, statement submitted to the Sidle Committee, January 30, 1984. Fritts is the president of the National Association of Broadcasters.

Chapter 2

1. Emmet Crozier, *American Reporters on the Western Front* (New York: Oxford University Press, 1959), pp. 279-80.
2. Peter Braestrup, *Big Story* (New Haven: Yale University Press, 1983), pp. 20-22.
3. Meyer Berger, *The Story of the New York Times, 1851-1951* (New York: Arno Press, 1970), pp. 510-24.

4. Robert Sherrod, *Tarawa* (Fredericksburg, Texas: Admiral Nimitz Foundation, 1973).

5. John Hohenberg, *Foreign Correspondents: The Great Reporters and Their Times* (New York: Columbia University Press, 1964), pp. 367-68.

6. Palmer Hoyt, "The Use and Abuse of Restraints," in *Journalism in Wartime,* ed. Frank Luther Mott (Washington, D.C.: American Council on Public Affairs, 1943), pp. 34-43.

7. Harry C. Butcher, *My Three Years with Eisenhower* (New York: Simon and Schuster, 1946), p. 670.

8. See Lloyd J. Graybar, "Admiral King's Toughest Battle," *Naval War College Review,* February 1979; cited in Jack A. Gottschalk, "Consistent with Security: A History of American Military Press Censorship," in *Communications and the Law,* Summer 1983.

9. David E. Scherman, ed., *LIFE Goes to War* (New York: Time-Life Films, 1977), p. 131.

10. Ralph H. Turner, "Photographers in Uniform," in *Journalism in Wartime,* ed. Frank Luther Mott (Washington, D.C.: American Council on Public Affairs, 1943), pp. 77-82. Mott is the dean of the School of Journalism at the University of Missouri.

11. Ibid.

12. See Dwight D. Eisenhower, *Crusade in Europe* (New York: Doubleday, 1948); Butcher, *My Three Years with Eisenhower.*

13. See John MacVane, *On the Air in World War II* (New York: William Morrow and Co., 1979).

14. Personal correspondence from Brigadier General Robert A. McClure to Sir Cyril Radcliffe, February 9, 1944. National Archives, Record Group 331, Records of Allied Operational and Occupational Headquarters, World War II, Supreme Headquarters Allied Expeditionary Force (SHAEF), Secretary General Staff (SGS), Decimal File 000.74.

15. Minutes of meeting at Supreme Headquarters Allied Expeditionary Force (SHAEF), Public Relations Division, 170A Great Portland Street, London, April 24, 1944, p. 3, RG 331, SHAEF, SGS, Decimal File 1943-45, 000.73-2.

16. Ibid.

17. Memorandum to chief public relations officer, Publicity and Psychological Warfare, Supreme Headquarters Allied Expeditionary Force, from Major Fred M. Payne (Canada), March 20, 1944, pp. 1-2, SHAEF, SGS, Decimal File 000.73.

18. Memorandum to the chief of staff, Publicity and Psychological Warfare, Supreme Headquarters Allied Expeditionary Force, from Brigadier General Robert A. McClure, April 12, 1944. RG 331, SHAEF, SGS, Decimal File 000.7-1.

19. Ibid.

20. Brigadier General Robert A. McClure, memorandum to Lieutenant

General Walter Bedell Smith, April 12, 1944. RG 331, SHAEF, Public Relations Division (PRD), Decimal File 000.7-1.

21. Personal correspondence with Drew Middleton, September 5, 1984.

22. Public Relations Plan "Overlord," SHAEF, Public Relations Division, May 1, 1944. SHAEF, SGS, Decimal File May 1943-August 1945, 381/9, Overlord PRD.

23. Ibid.

24. Ibid., app. A.

25. Lieutenant General Walter Bedell Smith, operational memorandum on press censorship, April 18, 1944. SHAEF, SGS, Decimal File 000.73.

26. "Notes for War Correspondents Accredited to SHAEF" (n.d.). RG 331, SHAEF, SGS, Decimal File 000.73, Volume I.

27. Brigadier General Thomas Jefferson Davis, "War Correspondents Concerning When Some Question Has Arisen" (memorandum to Lieutenant General Walter Bedell Smith, April 25, 1944). SHAEF, SGS, Decimal File 000.74.

28. Ibid.

29. See Eisenhower address, May 11, 1944, Supreme Headquarters Allied Expeditionary Force file. SHAEF, SGS, Decimal File 000.74.

30. "Suggestions for Gen. Smith's Talk," SHAEF file, no date. RG 331, SHAEF, SGS, May 1943-August 1945, Decimal File 000.74, Volume I.

31. "Press Thanks Gen. Davis," *New York Times,* May 7, 1944, p. 14.

32. James MacDonald, "Invasion Newsmen Hope for 'Breaks,'" *New York Times,* May 27, 1944, p. 2.

33. Ibid.

34. The others included Sonya Tomara of the *New York Herald Tribune* and Walter Cronkite's competitor from International News Service, Dixie Tighe. Cronkite was not assigned to go ashore with the First U.S. Army troops at Omaha and Utah beaches. There the United Press chores were handled by two other men: W. H. Higginbotham and one F. McGlincy. The *New York Times* sent Harold Denney with the Twenty-first Army Group along with Charles Collingwood of CBS, who was with the navy.

35. Among the others in London were Drew Middleton and Raymond Daniell for the *New York Times,* Mary Welsh for *Time* magazine, and William S. White for the Associated Press.

36. The twenty who were assigned to land with the U.S. forces on D-Day were J. F. King and E. D. Ball (Associated Press); W. H. Higginbotham and F. McGlincy (United Press); Clark Lee, Richard Tregaskis, and L. Azrael (International News Service); B. Stoneman (*Chicago Daily News*); J. Thompson (*Chicago Tribune*); B. Brandt (Still Pool [Acme]); H. P. Andrews (Acme News Pictures); P. Carroll and Harry Harris (Associated Press Photo Service); G. K. Hodenfield (*Stars*

& Stripes); John MacVane (NBC); Larry Lesueur (CBS); G. E. Hicks (Blue Network); J. O'Reilly (*New York Herald Tribune*); N. Sullivan (U.S. Newsreel Pool); A. J. Liebling (*The New Yorker*).

37. See "Accrediting of War Correspondents to SHAEF" (Memorandum to chief of staff, SHAEF, from Brigadier General Robert A. McClure, March 22, 1944). SHAEF, SGS, Decimal File 000.74.

38. Lieutenant General Walter Bedell Smith, "Calling Up of Press Correspondents to Witness 'OVERLORD'" (Memorandum to the secretary, Chiefs of Staff Committee, Offices of the War Cabinet, June 2, 1944). SHAEF, SGS, Decimal File 000.74.

39. Ibid.

40. Leonard Mosley, "Witness Depicts Leap of 'Chutists,'" *New York Times,* June 9, 1944, p. 5.

41. "U.S. Beachhead Reporter Says News System Failed," *New York Times,* June 10, 1944, p. 4.

42. "2,500,000 Words Cabled Since Start of Invasion," *New York Times,* June 11, 1944, p. 34.

43. John MacVane, *On the Air in World War II* (New York: William Morrow and Co., 1979), p. 208.

44. Ibid., p. 215.

45. Ibid., p. 247.

46. E. C. Daniel, "Allies' Censorship Works with Speed," *New York Times,* June 14, 1944, p. 4.

47. "Invasion Newsmen Form Press Relations Unit," *New York Times,* July 9, 1944, p. 4. Other committee members were Herbert Clark, Blue Network (radio); Don Whitehead, Associated Press correspondent (news services); Montague Lacey, *The London Daily Express* (British); Harry Harris, Associated Press (photographers); A. J. Liebling, *The New Yorker* (magazines).

48. Personal correspondence, Colonel R. Ernest Depuy to Major General C.M.F. White, July 12, 1944. RG 331, SHAEF, Public Relations Division, Decimal File 000.7-1.

49. William Hickey, "No Flash Back," *Daily Express* (London), July 29, 1944.

50. Drew Middleton recalls: "Once we left London, we were told Dieppe was the objective. Mountbatten openly described [the] operation as a failure, supporting reports from battle." From personal correspondence, September 5, 1984.

51. Joe Alex Morris, "The European Invasion Front," in *Journalism in Wartime,* ed. Frank Luther Mott (Washington, D.C.: American Council on Public Affairs, 1943).

52. 'Softening Up' the Western Coast," *New York Times,* May 28, 1944, p. E1.

53. Colonel William P. Nuckols, memorandum to Ninth Air Force

Public Relations Officer (no title), May 27, 1944. RG 331, SHAEF, Public Relations Division, Decimal File 1943-45, 000.73-2.

54. "Latest Invasion Called War's Most Open Secret," *New York Times,* August 16, 1944, p. 4.

55. "President to Ease Curb on War News," *New York Times,* February 18, 1944, p. 3.

56. Ibid.

57. Ibid.

58. Butcher, *My Three Years with Eisenhower,* p. 362.

59. Eric Sevareid, *Not So Wild a Dream* (New York: Alfred A. Knopf, 1946), pp. 388-89.

60. Ibid., pp. 494-95.

Chapter 3

1. See W. J. Koenig, *Americans at War* (New York: G. P. Putnam's Sons, 1980), chap. 9.

2. Ibid.

3. John Hohenberg, *Foreign Correspondence: The Great Reporters and Their Times* (New York: Columbia University Press, 1964), p. 390.

4. Ibid., pp. 390-91. The most notable among the World War II veteran reporters were Associated Press's Don Whitehead, Relman Morin, Hal Boyle, and Robert Eunson; Homer Bigart from the *New York Herald Tribune* and Robert Vermillion of the United Press; also Jim Lucas of the Scripps-Howard newspaper, and Marguerite Higgins of the *New York Herald Tribune.*

5. Narrative Historical Report, General Headquarters, United Nations Command-Far East Command, Supreme Commander Allied Powers (SCAP), January 1-October 31, 1950.

6. Telephone interview with Howard Handleman, March 26, 1984.

7. "MacArthur Cancels Ban on Reporters," *New York Times,* July 16, 1950, p. 7.

8. Ibid.

9. Ibid.

10. "Command and Press Relationships in the Korean Conflict," prepared for the House Subcommittee on Foreign Operating and Government Information, by B. C. Mossman, Office of the Chief of Military History, no date, p. 3. See also Melvin B. Voorhees, *Korean Tales* (New York: Simon and Schuster, 1952), pp. 103-4. Colonel Voorhees was an Eighth Army censor.

11. Karl A. Von Voigtlander, "The War for Words," *Army Information Digest 8* (1953), pp. 54-59; cited by Mossman, "Command and Press Relationships in the Korean Conflict." Major Von Voigtlander was a censor for the Far East Command.

12. Telephone interview with Keyes Beech, March 26, 1984.

13. Telephone interview with Howard Handleman, March 26, 1984.

14. "Situation Not Normal," *Newsweek,* September 25, 1950, p. 61.

15. Personal correspondence with Keyes Beech, March 12, 1984; telephone interviews with Beech, March 26, 1984, and Howard Handleman, March 26, 1984.

16. Von Voigtlander, "The War for Words"; cited by Mossman, "Command and Press Relationships in the Korean Conflict."

17. Ibid.

18. Ibid.

19. Mossman, "Command and Press Relationships in the Korean Conflict," p. 8. See also Voorhees, *Korean Tales.*

20. Mossman, "Command and Press Relationships in the Korean Conflict."

21. Ibid., p. 9. See also "Censorship Criteria," Press Advisory Division, Public Information Office, General Headquarters, Far East Command, August 1951; Colonel M. P. Echols, "Information in the Combat Zone," *Army Information Digest,* 6 (1951), pp. 60-4; Von Voigtlander, "The War for Words"; Noble J. Wiley, Jr., "The Pen Supports the Sword," *Army Information Digest* 8 (1953), pp. 7-13. Colonel Wiley was Eighth Army public information officer at this time.

22. Mossman, "Command and Press Relationships in the Korean Conflict," p. 10. See also Voorhees, *Korean Tales,* pp. 106-7.

23. Mossman, "Command and Press Relationships," p. 11.

24. Far East Command Monthly Command Report (available at the General Services Administration Federal Records Center, Alexandria, VA), January 1951; cited by Mossman, "Command and Press Relationships in the Korean Conflict."

25. Memorandum, Public Information Office, General Headquarters, Far East Command, to all correspondents, March 17, 1951; cited by Mossman, "Command and Press Relationships in the Korean Conflict," p. 13.

26. Far East Command Monthly Command Report, March 1951; Von Voigtlander, "The War for Words"; cited by Mossman, "Command and Press Relationships in the Korean Conflict," p. 13.

27. Ibid.

28. Wiley, "The Pen Supports the Sword"; Von Voigtlander, "The War for Words"; cited by Mossman, "Command and Press Relationships in the Korean Conflict."

29. Far East Command Report, June 1951; Von Voigtlander, "The War for Words"; cited by Mossman, "Command and Press Relationships in the Korean Conflict."

30. Von Voigtlander, "The War for Words"; Voorhees, *Korean Tales;* cited by Mossman, "Command and Press Relationships in the Korean Conflict."

31. Mossman, "Command and Press Relationships in the Korean Conflict," p. 16.

32. Ibid., pp. 16-17. See also, "Path to Panmunjom Smoothed by Reds' Show of Compromise," *Newsweek,* October 29, 1951, pp. 28-30.

33. Mossman, "Command and Press Relationships in the Korean Conflict," p. 17.

34. Ibid., pp. 16-17.

35. Quoted from Check Sheet, Public Information Office to C/S, February 3, 1952; cited by Mossman, "Command and Press Relationships in the Korean Conflict."

36. Far East Command Monthly Command Report, January 1952; cited by Mossman, "Command and Press Relationships in the Korean Conflict," p. 22.

37. Far East Command Monthly Command Report, February 1952; cited by Mossman, "Command and Press Relationships in the Korean Conflict," p. 22.

38. Mossman, "Command and Press Relationships in the Korean Conflict," p. 23.

39. Far East Command Monthly Command Report, May 1952; cited by Mossman, "Command and Press Relationships in the Korean Conflict," p. 25. But Howard Handleman and Keyes Beech recall that this story broke in much less than a month (from personal correspondence, September 8, 1984, letter and February 15, 1985, phone conversation, respectively).

40. Ibid.

41. Mossman, "Command and Press Relationships in the Korean Conflict," p. 27.

Chapter 4

1. Robert Elegant, "How to Lose a War," *Encounter,* August 1981.

2. See, for example, William Small, *To Kill a Messenger* (New York: Hastings House, 1970).

3. See, for example, Peter Braestrup, *Big Story* (New Haven: Yale University Press, 1983), p. xi.

4. Richard Betts, "Misadventure Revisited," *Vietnam as History,* ed. Peter Braestrup (Washington, D.C.: University Press of America, 1984), p. 3.

5. Cited during hearings of 89th Congress, Second Session, U.S. Senate Committee on Foreign Relations, August 31, 1966, "News Policies in Vietnam," p. 64.

6. Ibid.

7. Ibid.

8. Ibid.

9. Testimony of Arthur Sylvester, assistant secretary of defense for public affairs, during hearings of the 89th Congress, Second Session, U.S. Senate Committee on Foreign Relations, August 31, 1966, "News Policies in Vietnam," pp. 66-67.

10. Ibid., p. 73.

11. *Vietnam: 10 Years Later* (Defense Information School, Ft. Benjamin Harrison, Indiana, 1984), p. 52.

12. See Peter Braestrup, *Big Story,* pp. 239, 557.

13. *Vietnam: 10 Years Later,* p. 67.

14. Ibid., p. 65-66.

15. Second declaration of Michael Burch, assistant secretary of defense for public affairs, *Flynt v. Weinberger* No. 83-3191 (D.C. Circ. 1984).

16. Testimony of Arthur Sylvester, August 31, 1966, pp. 76-77.

17. Article cited by Senator J. W. Fulbright, chairman, during hearings of the 89th Congress, Second Session, U.S. Senate Committee on Foreign Relations, August 31, 1966, "News Policies in Vietnam," pp. 79-80.

18. William Westmoreland, *A Soldier Reports* (New York: Doubleday, 1976), pp. 420.

19. Elegant, "How to Lose a War."

20. Lawrence W. Lichty, "Comments on the Influence of Television on Public Opinion," *Vietnam as History,* ed. Peter Braestrup (Washington, D.C.: University Press of America, 1984).

21. Michael Arlen, "The Falklands, Vietnam, and Our Collective Memory," *The New Yorker,* August 16, 1982.

22. John Mueller, "A Summary of Public Opinion and the Vietnam War," *Vietnam as History,* ed. Peter Braestrup (Washington, D.C.: University Press of America, 1984).

23. Douglas Kinnard, *The War Managers* (Hanover, N.H.: University Press of New England, 1977), p. 175.

24. *Vietnam: 10 Years Later,* p. 86.

25. *New York Times,* July 13, 1970, p. 3.

26. *New York Times,* April 13, 1972, p. 11.

27. See Don Oberdorfer's *Tet!* (DaCapo Press, 1984), Herbert Schandler's *Lyndon Johnson and Vietnam* (Princeton, 1983), and Peter Braestrup's *Big Story,* among other analyses of the period.

Chapter 5

1. See Kennett Love, *Suez: The Twice-Fought War* (New York: McGraw-Hill, 1969).

2. See George Russell, "Face-Off on the High Seas," *Time,* April 19, 1982, pp. 26-37; "Britannia Scorns to Yield," *Newsweek,* April 19, 1982, pp. 40-46.

3. Arthur A. Humphries, "Two Routes to the Wrong Destination: Public Affairs in the South Atlantic War," *Naval War College Review,* June 1983, p. 60. Humphries is a lieutenant commander in the navy.

4. Ibid., p. 59.

5. Ibid., p. 62.

6. Ibid.

7. Ibid., p. 60.

8. *Sunday Times* of London Insight Team, "The Other Casualty," *War in the Falklands* (New York: Harper and Row, 1982), pp. 225-26.

9. Ibid., p. 227.

10. "Misled on Falklands, British Press Says," *New York Times,* July 29, 1983, p. A3.

11. Ibid.

12. *Sunday Times* of London Insight Team, "The Other Casualty," p. 225.

13. Ibid., pp. 225-26.

14. Gerald Clarke, "Covering an Uncoverable War," *Time,* May 17, 1983, p.53.

15. John Leo, "A War Ever Tougher to Cover," *Time,* May 24, 1982, p. 70.

16. William Borders, "Impartial Coverage of Crisis Infuriating Some In Britain," *New York Times,* May 11, 1982, p. A6.

17. Jerry Adler and Tony Clifton, "In War, Truth or Faction?" *Newsweek,* May 24, 1982, p. 86.

18. Humphries, "Two Routes to the Wrong Destination," p. 71.

19. Thomas Collins, "Did Navy Article Foretell U.S. Press on Grenada?" *Newsday,* December 11, 1983, p. 9.

20. See, for example, Janice Castro, "Keeping the Press from the Action," *Time,* November 7, 1983, p. 65; "White House Admits Pentagon Censorship," *Baltimore Sun,* October 28, 1983, p. 10.

Chapter 6

1. See "'U.S. Had to Act Strongly, Decisively,'" *Washington Post,* October 26, 1983, p. A7.

2. Mark Whitaker, "A Crisis in the Caribbean," *Newsweek,* October 31, 1983, pp. 40-41.

3. "The Invasion of Grenada," *Washington Post,* October 26, 1983, p. A7.

4. Ralph Kinney Bennett, "Grenada: Anatomy of a 'Go' Decision," *Reader's Digest,* February 1984, pp. 72-77.

5. "U.S. Invades Grenada, Fights Cubans," *Washington Post,* October 26, 1983.

6. "News Conference by Secretary of Defense Caspar W. Weinberger and General John W. Vessey, Jr., U.S. Army, chairman, Joint Chiefs of Staff, at the Pentagon," October 26, 1983, p. 7.

7. Ed Magnuson, "D-Day in Grenada," *Time,* November 7, 1983, p. 22.

8. Gerald F. Seib, "No More 'Micromanagement' of the Military," *Wall Street Journal,* November 8, 1983, p. 34.

9. See "Transcript of Shultz News Conference on Invasion of Grenada," *New York Times,* October 26, 1983, p. A18.

10. Frank J. Prial, "U.S. Envoy Traveling to Grenada to Check on Safety of Americans," *New York Times,* October 23, 1983, p. 1.

11. Edward Cody, "Grenada Sanction Discussed," *Washington Post,* October 23, 1983, p. 1. Cody did not list the leaders or their countries.

12. Ibid.

13. Edward Cody, "Grenada Puts Military on Alert, Warns of U.S. Threat to Invade," *Washington Post,* October 24, 1983, p. A4.

14. Fred Hiatt, "U.S. Flotilla Remains Near Grenada after Lebanon Bombings," *Washington Post,* October 25, 1983, p. A14.

15. Michael Kernan, "Picturing the Invasion," *Washington Post,* October 26, 1983, p. B1.

16. "U.S. Troops Remove 4 Reporters," *Washington Post,* October 27, 1983, p. A8; Edward Cody, "U.S. Forces Thwart Journalists' Reports," *Washington Post,* October 28, 1983, p. A16.

17. Cody, "U.S. Forces Thwart Journalists' Reports."

18. See Paul McIssac, "Revolutionary Suicide," *Village Voice,* November 22, 1983, pp. 11-14.

19. Lou Cannon and David Hoffman, "Invasion Secrecy Creating a Furor," *Washington Post,* October 27, 1983, p. A1.

20. Telephone interview with Colonel Robert O'Brien, U.S. Air Force, deputy assistant secretary of defense for public affairs, February 14, 1984.

21. Personal correspondence.

22. Cannon and Hoffman, "Invasion Secrecy Creating a Furor," p. A1.

23. Lois Romano, "The Truth and How to Avoid It," *Washington Post,* October 28, 1983, p. B3.

24. Personal correspondence from Bill Plante, March 30, 1985.

25. Lou Cannon, "Reagan Press Aide Resigns," *Washington Post,* November 1, 1983, p. A1.

26. Cannon and Hoffman, "Invasion Secrecy Creating a Furor."

27. Roy Gutman, "Deferring to the Military when It Comes to the Media," *Newsday,* November 4, 1984, p. 15.

28. Walter Scott, "Personality Parade," *Washington Post, Parade* magazine, January 15, 1984, p. 4.

29. B. Drummond Ayres, Jr., "Grenada Invasion: A Series of Surprises," *New York Times,* November 14, 1983, p. 1.

30. John J. Fialka, "In Battle for Grenada, Command Mission Didn't Go as Planned," *Wall Street Journal,* November 15, 1983, p. 1.

31. Ayres, "Grenada Invasion," p. 1.

32. Michael J. Byron, "Fury from the Sea: Marines in Grenada," *Pro-*

ceedings of U.S. Naval Institute, May 1984, pp. 118-31. Byron is a lieutenant colonel in the marines.

33. Ibid., and "Metcalf Praises Invasion Force, Describes Rescues of Civilians," *Navy Times,* advance release, November 21, 1983.

34. Hiatt, "U.S. Flotilla Remains Near Grenada," p. A14.

35. Stuart Taylor, Jr., "In the Wake of Invasion, Much Official Misinformation by U.S. Comes to Light," *New York Times,* November 6, 1983, p. A20.

36. News Conference by Admiral Wesley L. McDonald, USN "Commander-In-Chief, Atlantic Fleet, at the Pentagon," October 28, 1983.

37. "News Conference by Secretary of Defense Caspar W. Weinberger and General John W. Vessey, Jr., U.S. Army, chairman, Joint Chiefs of Staff, at the Pentagon," October 26, 1983, p. 5.

38. "Metcalf Praises Invasion Force, Describes Rescues of Civilians," *Navy Times,* advance release, November 21, 1983.

39. Kenneth Turner, "Admiral Fights 2 Battles: With Grenada and Press," *Washington Post,* October 31, 1983, p. 24.

40. "Metcalf Says Military People Have a Dislike for the Press," *Navy Times,* advance release, January 16, 1984.

41. Telephone interview with Captain Owen Resweber, chief public affairs officer for Atlantic Fleet/Atlantic Command, February 15, 1984.

42. Telephone interview with Major Donald Black, U.S. Air Force, operations chief, Joint Information Bureau, Bridgetown, Barbados, conducted by Mark Thompson, February 16, 1984.

43. Telephone interview with Colonel James Elmer, U.S. Air Force, commander of Aerospace Audio Visual Command, Norton Air Force Base, February 22, 1984.

44. Telephone interview with Captain Owen Resweber, February 15, 1984.

45. Ibid.

46. Telephone interview with Major Donald Black, February 16, 1984.

47. Interview with Commander Ronald Wildermuth, U.S. Navy, deputy public affairs officer for Atlantic Fleet/Atlantic Command, formerly director of Joint Information Bureau, Bridgetown, Barbados, February 16, 1984.

48. Ibid.

49. Telephone interview with Major Barry Willey, U.S. Army, chief public affairs officer for the 82nd Airborne Division, Fort Bragg, North Carolina, February 22, 1984.

50. Interview with Commander Ronald Wildermuth, February 16, 1984.

51. "Grenada," ABC memorandum from Steve Shepard to Ed Fouhy, ABC vice-president and Washington bureau chief, January 4, 1984.

52. Ibid.

53. "reMARKS" #22 (ABC newsletter), December 1983. Sandy Gilmour of CBS recalls: "The audio for pool, however, [was] not on my tape recorder; it [was] on the video tape machines (two of them, yet) and [could] not be transcribed until the tapes [were] played back at cable and wireless. I invited all radio people to cable and wireless; few showed up. The PIOs, after considerable persuasion, finally saw that reporters who wished to interview other reporters had plenty of print people to talk to, who were going over their notes, anyway. So Scheerer of ABC complains I won't share my audio at Barbados airport.... Again, this came about because PIOs did not control the pool, and in the last minute, before departing Barbados for the pool tour of Grenada, allow[ed] ABC and NBC both to come in as pools." From personal correspondence, September 18, 1984.

54. Thomas Ricks, personal correspondence, February 25, 1984.

55. Urgent Fury Public Affairs USCINCLANT Joint Information Bureau "Significant Events" (chronology of Grenada activities from October 27 to November 4, 1983), Department of Navy Public Affairs Office.

56. Dan Sewell, "Grenada All but Abandoned by the Media," *AP Log,* December 5, 1983.

57. Ed Cody's first story ("U.S. Forces Thwart Journalists' Reports," *Washington Post,* October 28, 1983) focused on his own experiences in St. George's and on the *Guam;* oddly, it did not give the reader any information on the operations of the marines whose officers Cody and his colleagues encountered near St. George's the morning of October 26. By contrast, as *Time's* Diederich pointed out to the author, he, the *Miami Herald's* Don Bohning, and *Newsday's* Morris Thompson all reported on the marine activities.

58. See Bernard Diederich, "What the Hell's Going on Here," *Dateline '84* (Overseas Press Club publication), May 1984, p. 11.

59. "News Update," *TV Guide,* November 5, 1983, p. A-1.

60. Tad Szulc, "Dominican War Keeps Times Troops Hopping," in *The Working Press,* ed. Ruth Adler (New York: G. P. Putnam's Sons, 1966), pp. 124-20.

61. Ayres, "Grenada Invasion," p. 1.

62. Jay Finegan, "Jumping Into a Hot DZ at 500 Feet," *Army Times,* November 14, 1983, p. 1.

63. Taylor, "In Wake of Invasion," p. A20.

64. See, for example, Richard Harwood, "Tidy U.S. War Ends: 'We Blew Them Away,'" *Washington Post,* November 6, 1983, p. A1; Ayres, "Grenada Invasion," p. A1; Fialka, "In Battle for Grenada, Command Mission Didn't Go as Planned," p. 1.

65. Mark Whitaker et al., "The Battle for Grenada," *Newsweek,* November 7, 1983, p. 66.

66. "Media Access to Grenada Stirs Controversy," *AP Log,* October 31, 1983, p. 1.

Chapter 7

1. David Hoffman, "Speakes Admits Possibility That He Misled Press," *Washington Post,* October 26, 1983, p. A11.
2. Transcript of press briefing by Larry Speakes, the Briefing Room, October 26, 1983, The White House, Office of the Press Secretary, p. 41.
3. Lou Cannon and David Hoffman, "Invasion Secrecy Creating a Furor," *Washington Post,* October 27, 1983, p. A1.
4. Ibid.
5. "News Conference by Secretary of Defense Caspar W. Weinberger and General John W. Vessey, Jr., U.S. Army, chairman, Joint Chiefs of Staff, at the Pentagon," October 26, 1983, p. 5.
6. Ibid.
7. Ibid.
8. David Bauman and David Fink, "Press Fights to Cover Invasion," *USA Today,* October 27, 1983, pp. 1A.
9. Cannon and Hoffman, "Invasion Secrecy Creating a Furor," p. A1.
10. NBC-TV, "NBC Nightly News," October 26, 1983.
11. ABC-TV, "Nightline," October 26, 1983.
12. Ibid.
13. Ibid.
14. WTOP Radio, "Dan Rather Commentary," October 27, 1983.
15. Tom Shales, "Grenada: A Question of News Control," *Washington Post,* October 28, 1983, p. B1.
16. "That Uncertain Feeling," *Los Angeles Times,* October 27, 1983, p. II6.
17. Janice Castro, "Keeping the Press from the Action," *Time,* November 7, 1983, p. 12.
18. Transcript of "Press briefing by Larry Speakes," Mr. Speakes's Office, October 28, 1983, The White House, Office of the Press Secretary, p. 12.
19. "Grenada—and Mount Suribachi," *New York Times,* October 28, 1983, p. A26.
20. Ibid.
21. Ibid.
22. "Censoring the Invasion," *Washington Post,* October 28, 1983, p. 22A.
23. "Reagan's Double Approach...and the First Casualty," *St. Louis Post-Dispatch,* October 28, 1983, p. 18A.
24. "'America First' Means Nothing to Selfish U.S. Press," *New York Post,* October 28, 1983, p. 7.

25. Reed Irvine, "What the Media Would Have Done," *Washington Inquirer*, December 2, 1983, p. 5.

26. Jeffrey Hart, "Military Justified in Barring Press," *Colorado Springs Gazette-Telegraph*, November 12, 1983, p. D8.

27. Charles Kaiser, Lucy Howard et al., "An Off-the-Record War," *Newsweek*, November 7, 1983, p. 83.

28. "The Secret War," *Army Times*, November 14, 1983, p. 23.

29. "The Administration's Continuing Effort to Bar Reporters and Manage News from Grenada," *Congressional Record*, Senate, 98th Congress, First Session, October 28, 1983, S14877.

30. "Press Banned in Grenada," *Congressional Record*, Extension of Remarks, 98th Congress, First Session, October 27, 1983, E5167.

31. Fred Hiatt and David Hoffman, "U.S. Drops Estimates of Cubans on Island," *Washington Post*, October 30, 1983, p. A1.

32. "Networks Take Censorship Complaints to Congress," *Broadcasting*, November 7, 1983, p. 36.

33. Statement of John Chancellor before 98th Congress, First Session, House Committee of the Judiciary, Subcommittee on Courts, Civil Liberties, and the Administration of Justice, November 2, 1983.

34. Statement of David Brinkley before the House Judiciary Subcommittee on Courts, Civil Liberties, and the Administration of Justice, November 2, 1983.

35. "Networks Take Censorship Complaints to Congress," *Broadcasting*, November 7, 1983, pp. 36-37.

36. David Burnham, "Curbs on Grenada News Coverage Criticized in House Hearings," *New York Times*, November 3, 1983, p. 21.

37. Jack Nelson, "Credibility Hurt in White House News Blackout," *Los Angeles Times*, November 7, 1983, p. 1.

38. Juan Williams, "Speakes Faults Leaving Media Out of Invasion," *Washington Post*, January 15, 1984, p. A19.

39. Jack Nelson, "Bare Majority Backs Grenada News Blackouts," *Los Angeles Times*, November 20, 1983, p. 1.

40. "Journalism Under Fire," *Time*, December 12, 1983, pp. 76-93.

41. William Schneider, "Despite Grenada, the Public Trusts the Press More than the Government," *National Journal*, February 4, 1984, p. 238.

42. Louis Harris, "Does the Public Really Hate the Press?" *Columbia Journalism Review*, March-April, 1983, p. 18.

43. "Statement of Ed Godfrey, RTNDA President on Restraint of News Media Coverage of the Invasion of Grenada," Washington, D.C., October 27, 1983.

44. Cited in "Reagan Press Policy on Grenada Criticized," *Baltimore Sun*, October 29, 1983, p. 3.

45. Published in part in "Editors Protest to Pentagon," *New York Times*, November 1, 1983, p. 16A.

46. See, for example, "Statement," Women in Communications, Inc., Austin, Texas, October 27, 1983.

47. Besides the Reporters Committee, the Socialist Workers and the American Civil Liberties Union considered filing suits. See Reporters Committee for Freedom of the Press, Washington, D.C., "Background Paper on Press Exclusion from Grenada," November 30, 1983, p. 11.

48. "Reporters Committee May Sue Government," *Editor & Publisher,* November 19, 1983, p. 16.

49. *Larry Flynt v. Caspar Weinberger,* "Complaint and Prayer for Declaratory and Injunctive Relief," Civil Action no. 83-3191, U.S. District Court for the District of Columbia, October 26, 1983.

50. Steven Helle, "Hustler and the First Amendment," *Editor & Publisher,* December 10, 1983, p. 52.

51. Jonathan Friendly, "Restraint of the Press," *New York Times,* December 4, 1983, p. 47.

52. Steven Helle, "Hustler and the First Amendment," *Editor & Publisher,* December 10, 1983, p. 52.

53. "Press Groups Ask Talks on Combat Coverage," *New York Times,* December 2, 1983, p. 11.

54. Benjamin W. Heineman, Jr., "Briefing Papers," November 28, 1983, sent to Jack Landau, executive director, Reporters Committee for Freedom of the Press, Washington, D.C.

55. "Press Groups Ask Talks on Combat Coverage," *New York Times,* December 2, 1983.

56. "Media Organizations Take a Stand," *Editor & Publisher,* January 14, 1984, p. 18.

57. John Consoli and Andrew Radoff, "Working with the White House," *Editor & Publisher,* January 21, 1984.

58. See "Media Organizations Take a Stand," *Editor & Publisher,* January 14, 1984.

59. "Working with the White House," *Editor & Publisher,* January 21, 1984.

60. Ibid.

61. Ibid.

62. "Press Groups Ask Talks on Combat Coverage," *New York Times,* December 2, 1983.

63. Reporters Committee for Freedom of the Press, "Background Paper," p. 11.

64. "Press Groups Ask Talks on Combat Coverage," *New York Times,* December 2, 1983.

65. Keith Fuller, statement submitted to the Chairman of the Joint Chiefs of Staff Panel on Media-Military Relations (the Sidle Committee), January 23, 1984.

66. Richard L. Harwood, statement submitted to the Sidle Committee, January 31, 1984. Harwood is deputy managing editor of the *Washington Post.*

67. Fuller, January 23, 1984.

68. Richard M. Smith, statement submitted to the Sidle Committee, January 24, 1984. Smith is Editor-in-chief of *Newsweek.*

69. William W. Headline, statement submitted to the Sidle Committee, January 27, 1984.

70. Fuller, January 23, 1984.

71. Jerry W. Freidheim, statement submitted to the Sidle Committee, January 11, 1984. Freidheim is the executive vice president of the American Newspaper Publishers Association, and former assistant secretary of defense for public affairs.

72. Hardwood, January 31, 1984.

73. Freidheim, January 11, 1984; Creed C. Black, statement submitted to the Sidle Committee, January 13, 1984. Black is the president of the American Society of Newspaper Editors.

74. Fuller, January 23, 1984.

75. See "Key Sections of Panel's Report on the Military and the Press," *New York Times,* August 24, 1984, p. A6.

76. Letter from General Winant Sidle to General John W. Vessey, Jr., August 23, 1984, preceding the final report of the Chairman of the Joint Chiefs of Staff Media-Military Relations Panel.

77. Statement by the secretary of defense, August 23, 1984, No. 450-84.

78. Richard Halloran, "Pentagon Forms War Press Pool; Newspaper Reporters Excluded," *New York Times,* October 11, 1984, p. A1.

79. Jack Landau, "Media Law Today," *Editor & Publisher,* December 10, 1983, p. 10.

80. Reporters Committee for Freedom of the Press, "Background Paper."

81. Ibid., p. 12.

82. Ibid., p. 2; "White Paper on Media Coverage of Military Operations," (Draft), prepared for the Reporters Committee for Freedom of the Press by Benjamin Heineman, Jr., December 5, 1983, p. 6 (sources cited).

83. Public Affairs Office interviews.

84. Reporters Committee for Freedom of the Press, "Background Paper," p. 7.

85. Ibid., p. 8.

86. "White Paper on Media Coverage," p. 9.

87. Reporters Committee on Freedom of the Press, "Background Paper," p. 6.

88. *Richmond Newspapers Inc. v. Virginia,* 100 S.Ct. 2814 (1980).

89. Ibid. at 2821.

90. Ibid. at 2826, 2827.

91. Ibid. at 2831.

92. Ibid. at 2825.

93. Ibid. at 2829.

94. Reporters Committee for Freedom of the Press, "Background Paper," p. 2.

95. "White Paper," p. 10.

96. Jack Landau, "Media Law Today," *Editor & Publisher,* December 10, 1983, p. 10.

97. Ibid.; Reporters Committee for Freedom of the Press, "Background Paper," p. 2.

98. *Richmond Newspapers Inc. v. Virginia,* 100 S.Ct. 2814 (1980).

99. *Saxbe v. The Washington Post Co.,* 417 U.S. 843 (1974).

100. *Pell v. Procunier,* 417 U.S. 817, 834 (1974). *Pell* was a companion case to *Saxbe,* declared "unconstitutionally indistinguishable" and decided on the same day. See *Saxbe v. The Washington Post Co.,* 417 U.S. 843 (1974).

101. *Pell v. Procunier,* 417 U.S. 817, 834 (1974), at 834.

102. *Gannett Co. v. DePasquale,* 443 U.S. 368 (1979).

103. *Richmond Newspapers Inc. v. Virginia,* 100 S.Ct. 2814 (1980).

104. See U.S. Constitution, Article II.

105. Benjamin W. Heineman, Jr., "Possible Derivation of Constitutional Right or Principle that the Media Should Be Present at Overt Military Operations," Briefing Paper Draft, November 30, 1983, p. 2.

106. *Zemel v. Rusk,* 381 U.S. 1 (1965).

107. *United States v. Curtiss-Wright Export Corp.,* 299 U.S. 304 (1936).

108. *New York Times v. United States,* 91 S.Ct. 2140 (1971).

109. Ibid. at 2143.

110. "Media Law Today," *Editor & Publisher,* December 10, 1983, p. 10.

111. Telephone conversation with E. Barrett Prettyman, March 14, 1984.

112. Telephone conversation with Jack Landau, March 9, 1984.

Chapter 8

1. Jeremiah O'Leary, "Raiding and Writing Don't Mix, Shultz Says," *Washington Times,* December 16, 1983, p. 1.

2. John E. Murray, "Journalists in the Press of Battle," letter to the editor, *Wall Street Journal,* November 4, 1983.

3. Morris Janowitz, *The Professional Soldier* (New York: Free Press, 1960).

4. Ibid.

5. Bengt Abrahamsson, "Elements of Military Conservatism: Traditional and Modern," in *On Military Ideology,* ed. Morris Janowitz and Jacques van Doorn (Belgium: Rotterdam University Press, 1971), p. 62.

6. Janowitz, *The Professional Soldier,* p. 231.

7. Ibid., p. 246.

8. Personal interview with Robert Lichter, April 25, 1984.

9. Ibid.

10. See Janowitz, *The Professional Soldier,* chapters 6 and 7.

11. James Boylan, "The News Media: Newspeople," *The Wilson Quarterly,* Special Issue (1982), pp. 71-85.

12. Lawrence W. Lichty, "The News Media: Video versus Print," *The Wilson Qaurterly,* Special Issue (1982), p. 52.

13. Roger Rosenblatt, "Journalism and the Larger Truth," *Time,* July 2, 1984, p. 88.

14. Joel Swerdlow, "Television in America: A Question of Impact," *The Wilson Quarterly* (Winter 1981), pp. 86-101.

15. Michael Arlen, *The Living Room War* (New York: Viking, 1969), p. 143.

16. S. Robert Lichter and Stanley Rothman, "Media and Business Elites," *Public Opinion,* October-November 1981, p. 42.

17. Edward Jay Epstein, *News from Nowhere* (New York: Random House Vintage Books, 1973), p. 214.

18. Herbert J. Gans, *Deciding What's News* (New York: Random House Vintage Books, 1980), p. 211.

19. Michael Robinson, "Just How Liberal Is the News? 1980 Revisited," *Public Opinion,* February-March 1983, pp. 55-60.

20. Thomas M. DeFrank, "Michael Deaver Rates the President's Press," *Washington Journalism Review,* April 1984, p. 24.

APPENDIX
The Report of the Sidle Panel

Letter to General John W. Vessey, Jr., from Major General Winant Sidle

August 23, 1984

General John W. Vessey, Jr.
Chairman, Joint Chiefs of Staff
The Pentagon, Room 2E872
Washington, D.C. 20301

Dear General Vessey:

As you requested, enclosed are the final report and recommendations of the Sidle Panel, together with pertinent enclosures. The panel is unanimous in its strong belief that implementation of the recommendations, both in fact and in spirit, by the appropriate military authorities will set the stage for arriving at workable solutions for media-military relations in future military operations. We also believe that these solutions will be satisfactory to reasonable members of both the media and the military.

The report has three sections: an introduction, a recommendations section, and a comment section. We adopted this format because, while we were unanimous on the recommendations, there were some differences of opinion on some points in the comments. However, we all agreed that the comments were necessary to help explain the recommendations and that even the points on which we were not unanimous were worthy of consideration as suggestions and background for those who will implement the recommendations, should they be implemented. In any case, the entire panel has formally endorsed the recommendations, while I signed the comments. I should add that, where appropriate, I have mentioned the panel's degree of support in the comments.

The panel asked that I put three points in this letter that were not exactly germane to the report but required some comment on our part.

First, the matter of so-called First Amendment rights. This is an extremely gray area and the panel felt that it was a matter for the legal profession and the courts and that we were not qualified to provide a judgment. We felt justified in setting aside the issue, as we unanimously agreed at the outset that the U.S. media should cover U.S. military operations to the maximum degree possible consistent with mission security and the safety of U.S. forces.

Second, Grenada. We realize that Grenada had shown the need to review media-military relations in connection with military operations, but you did not request our assessment of media handling at Grenada and we will not provide it. However, we do feel that had our recommendations been "in place" and fully considered at the time of Grenada, there might have been no need to create our panel.

Finally, the matter of responsibility of the media. Although this is touched on in the report, and there is no doubt that the news organization representatives who appeared before us fully recognized their responsibilities, we feel we should state emphatically that reporters and editors alike must exercise responsibility in covering military operations. As one of the senior editors who appeared before us said, "The media must cover military operations comprehensively, intelligently, and objectively." The American people deserve news coverage of this quality and nothing less. It goes without saying, of course, that the military also has a concurrent responsibility, that of making it possible for the media to provide such coverage.

The members of the panel have also asked me to express their appreciation for being asked to participate in this important study and their hope that our work will be of value to the military, the media, and to the American people.

Finally, the panel considers this covering letter an integral part of our report.

Sincerely,

Winant Sidle
Major General, USA, Retired
Chairman

Enclosure
Report

INTRODUCTION

The Chairman of the Joint Chiefs of Staff (CJCS) Media-Military Relations Panel (known as the Sidle Panel) was created at the request of the Chairman, General John W. Vessey, Jr., who asked that I convene a panel of experts to make recommendations to him on, "How do we conduct military operations in a manner that safeguards the lives of our military and protects the security of the operation while keeping the American public informed through the media?"

Major General Winant Sidle, USA, Retired, was selected as chairman of this project and asked to assemble a panel composed of media representatives, public affairs elements of the four Military Services, the Office of the Assistant Secretary of Defense (Public Affairs) (OASD[PA]), and operations spokesmen from the Organization of the Joint Chiefs of Staff (OJCS).

The initial plan, concurred in by CJCS and ASD(PA), was to invite major umbrella media organizations and the Department of Defense organizations to provide members of this panel. The umbrella organizations, such as the American Newspaper Publishers Association (ANPA), the American Society of Newspaper Editors (ASNE), the National Association of Broadcasters (NAB), and the Radio-Television News Directors Association (RTNDA), and their individual member news organizations decided that they would cooperate fully with the panel but would not provide members. The general reason given was that it was inappropriate for media members to serve on a government panel.

This decision, unanimous among the major news media organizations, resulted in a revised plan calling for the non-military membership of the panel to be composed of experienced retired media personnel and representatives of schools of journalism who were experts in military-media relations. The Department of Defense organizations involved agreed to provide members from the outset. . . .*

To provide initial input to the panel for use as a basis for discussion when the panel met, a questionnaire was devised with the concurrence of CJCS and ASD(PA) and mailed to all participants. It was also sent to a number of additional organizations and individuals who had expressed interest and to some who had not but were considered to be experts in the matter. As the result of these mailings, the panel had available 24 written inputs to study prior to meeting. Of these, 16 were from major news organizations or umbrella groups. . . . The panel regretted that all who indicated interest could not appear before it, but time did not permit.

---

*Ellipses always indicate deleted references to material appended to the original Report of the Sidle Panel. The text was not cut.

Although the news organizations involved did not agree to provide panel members, they all agreed to provide qualified personnel to make oral presentations to the panel. The only exception was an individual news organization which felt that its umbrella group should represent it.

The panel met from 6 February through 10 February 1984 at the National Defense University, Fort McNair, Washington, D.C. The meetings included three days for media and military presentations in open sessions and two days for panel study and deliberation in closed session. The presentations included those by 25 senior media representatives speaking for 19 news organizations, including umbrella organizations. The chiefs/directors of Public Affairs for the Army, Navy, and Air Force also made major presentations during the open sessions with the USMC, OJCS, and ASD(PA) panel members making informal comments during the closed sessions. The open sessions were covered by about 70 reporters representing nearly 30 news organizations. . . .

The attached panel report is composed of two sections.

1. The Recommendations section, concurred and signed by all panel members.

2. The Comment section, explaining the recommendations and including comments, when appropriate, made by all concerned, to include both written and oral inputs to the committee and by the panel itself. This section is signed by the chairman but was approved unless otherwise indicated by the members of the panel. It is made available to explain the recommendations and to assist, via suggestions, in their implementation.

The panel recommends approval and implementation both in fact and in spirit of the recommendations made in Section I of this report.

Winant Sidle
Major General, USA, Retired
Chairman

Enclosure
Report

Report by
CJCS MEDIA-MILITARY RELATIONS PANEL
(SIDLE PANEL)

Section I: Recommendations

Statement of Principle

The American people must be informed about United States military operations and this information can best be provided through both the news media and the Government. Therefore, the panel believes it is essential that the U.S. news media cover U.S. military operations to the maximum degree possible consistent with mission security and the safety of U.S. forces.

This principle extends the major "Principles of Information" promulgated by the Secretary of Defense on 1 December 1983, which said:

> It is the policy of the Department of Defense to make available timely and accurate information so that the public, Congress, and members representing the press, radio and television may assess and understand the facts about national security and defense strategy. Requests for information from organizations and private citizens will be answered responsively and as rapidly as possible. . . ."

It should be noted that the above statement is in consonance with similar policies publicly stated by most former secretaries of defense.

The panel's statement of principle is also generally consistent with the first two paragraphs contained in "A Statement of Principle on Press Access to Military Operations" issued on 10 January 1984 by 10 major news organizations. . . . These were:

> First, the highest civilian and military officers of the government should reaffirm the historic principle that American journalists, print and broadcast, with their professional equipment, should be present at U.S. military operations. And the news media should reaffirm their recognition of the importance of U.S. military mission security and troop safety. When essential, both groups can agree on coverage conditions which satisfy safety and security imperatives while, in keeping with the spirit of the First Amendment, permitting independent reporting to the citizens of our free and open society to whom our government is ultimately accountable.

> Second, the highest civilian and military officers of the U.S. government should reaffirm that military plans should include planning for press access, in keeping with past traditions. The expertise of government public affairs officers during the planning of recent Grenada military operations could have met the interests of both the military and the press, to everyone's benefit.

Application of the panel's principle should be adopted both in substance and in spirit. This will make it possible better to meet the needs of both the military and the media during future military operations. The following recommendations by the panel are designed to help make this happen. They are primarily general in nature in view of the almost endless number of variations in military operations that could occur. However, the panel believes that they provide the necessary flexibility and broad guidance to cover almost all situations.

Recommendation 1:

That public affairs planning for military operations be conducted concurrently with operational planning. This can be assured in the great majority of cases by implementing the following:

a. Review all joint planning documents to assure that JCS guidance in public affairs matters is adequate.

b. When sending implementing orders to Commanders in Chief in the field, direct CINC planners to include consideration of public information aspects.

c. Inform the Assistant Secretary of Defense (Public Affairs) of an impending military operation at the earliest possible time. This information should appropriately come from the Secretary of Defense.

d. Complete the plan, currently being studied, to include a public affairs planning cell in OJCS to help ensure adequate public affairs review of CINC plans.

e. Insofar as possible and appropriate, institutionalize these steps in written guidance or policy.

Recommendation 2:

When it becomes apparent during military operational planning that news media pooling provides the only feasible means of furnishing the media with early access to an operation, planning should provide for the largest possible press pool that is practical and minimize the length of time the pool will be necessary before "full coverage" is feasible.

Recommendation 3:

That, in connection with the use of pools, the Joint Chiefs of Staff recommend to the Secretary of Defense that he study the matter of whether to use a pre-established and constantly updated accreditation or notification list of correspondents in case of a military operation for which a pool is required or the establishment of a news agency list for use in the same circumstances.

Recommendation 4:

That a basic tenet governing media access to military operations should be voluntary compliance by the media with security guidelines or ground rules established and issued by the military. These rules should be as few as possible and should be worked out during the planning process for each operation. Violations would mean exclusion of the correspondent(s) concerned from further coverage of the operation.

Recommendation 5:

Public Affairs planning for military operations should include sufficient equipment and qualified military personnel whose function is to assist correspondents in covering the operation adequately.

Recommendation 6:

Planners should carefully consider media communications requirements to assure the earliest feasible availability. However, these communications must not interfere with combat and combat support operations. If necessary and feasible, plans should include communications facilities dedicated to the news media.

Recommendation 7:

Planning factors should include provision for intra- and inter-theater transportation support of the media.

Recommendation 8:

To improve media-military understanding and cooperation:

a. CJCS should recommend to the Secretary of Defense that a program be undertaken by ASD(PA) for top military public affairs representatives to meet with news organization leadership, to include meetings with individual news organizations, on a reasonably regular basis to discuss mutual problems, including relationships with the media during military operations and exercises. This program should begin as soon as possible.

b. Enlarge programs already underway to improve military understanding of the media via public affairs instruction in service schools, to include media participation when possible.

c. Seek improved media understanding of the military through more visits by commanders and line officers to news organizations.

d. CJCS should recommend that the Secretary of Defense host at an early date a working meeting with representatives of the broadcast news media to explore the special problems of ensuring military security when and if there is real-time or near real-time news media audiovisual coverage of a battlefield and, if special problems exist, how they can best be dealt with consistent with the basic principle set forth at the beginning of this section of the report.

The panel members fully support the statement of principle and the supporting recommendations listed above and so indicate by their signatures below:

Winant Sidle, CHAIRMAN
   Major General, USA, Retired
Brent Baker, *Captain, USN*
Keyes Beech
Scott M. Cutlip
John T. Halbert
Billy Hunt
George Kirschenbauer, *Colonel, USA*

A. J. Langguth
Fred C. Lash, *Major, USMC*
James Major, *Captain, USN*
Wendell S. Merick
Robert O'Brien, *Colonel, USAF,*
   Deputy Assistant Secretary of Defense (Public Affairs)
Richard S. Salant
Barry Zorthian

Section II

Recommendation 1:

That public affairs planning for military operations be conducted concurrently with operational planning. This can be assured in the great majority of cases by implementing the following:

a. Review all joint planning documents to assure that JCS guidance in public affairs matters is adequate.

b. When sending implementing orders to Commanders in Chief in the field, direct that the CINC planners include consideration of public information aspects.

c. Inform the Assistant Secretary of Defense (Public Affairs) of an impending military operation at the earliest possible time. This information should appropriately come from the Secretary of Defense.

d. Complete the plan, currently being studied, to include a public affairs planning cell in OJCS to help ensure adequate public affairs review of CINC plans.

e. Insofar as possible and appropriate, institutionalize these steps in written guidance or policy.

Comments

1. Under the current system of planning for military operations, provisions exist to include public affairs planning but it is neither mandatory nor certain that current joint planning documents are adequate from a public affairs standpoint. The basic purpose of this recommendation is to help assure that public affairs aspects are considered as soon as possible in the planning cycle for any appropriate military operation and that the public affairs planning guidance is adequate.

2. The panel was unanimous in feeling that every step should be taken to ensure public affairs participation in planning and/or review at every appropriate level. Recommendations 1a, b, and d are designed to assist in implementing this consideration.

3. Panel discussions indicated that it is difficult to determine in advance in all cases when public affairs planning should be included. The panel felt that the best procedure would be to include such planning if there were even a remote chance it would be needed. For example, a strictly covert operation, such as the Son Tay raid in North Vietnam, still requires addressing public affairs considerations if only to be sure that after action coverage adequately fulfills the obligation to inform the American people. Very small, routine operations might be exceptions.

4. Recommendation 1c is self-explanatory. The ASD(PA), as the principal public affairs adviser to both the Secretary of Defense and the Chairman, JCS, must be brought into the planning process as soon as possible. In view of the DoD organization, the panel felt that this should be the responsibility of the Secretary of Defense.

5. We received indications that some commanders take the position that telling something to his public affairs officer is tantamount to telling it to the media. All members of the panel, including its public affairs officers decried this tendency and pointed out that a public affairs specialist is the least likely to release material prematurely to the media. Although the panel did not consider the matter officially, there is no doubt that public affairs officers are just as dedicated to maintaining military security as are operations officers and must know what is going on in a command if they are to do their job!

Recommendation 2:

When it becomes apparent during military operational planning that news media pooling provides the only feasible means of furnishing the media with early access to an operation, planning should support the largest possible press pool that is practical and minimize the length of time the pool will be necessary.

Comments

1. Media representatives appearing before the panel were unanimous in being opposed to pools in general. However, they all also agreed that they would cooperate in pooling agreements if that were necessary for them to obtain early access to an operation.

2. The media representatives generally felt that DoD should select the organizations to participate in pools, and the organizations should select the individual reporters. (See Recommendation 3.)

3. The media were unanimous in requesting that pools be terminated as soon as possible and "full coverage" allowed. "Full coverage" appeared to be a relative term, and some agreed that even this might be limited in cases where security, logistics, and the size of the operation created limitations that would not permit any and all bona fide reporters to cover an event. The panel felt that any limitations would have to be decided on a case-by-case basis but agreed that maximum possible coverage should be permitted.

4. The media agreed that prior notification of a pooling organization should be as close to H-Hour as possible to minimize the possibility of a story breaking too soon, especially if speculative stories about the operation should appear in media not in the pool or be initiated by one of their reporters not privy to the pool. This would require a pool media decision as to whether to break the story early, despite the embargo on such a break that is inherent in early notification for pooling purposes. The media representatives were not in agreement on this matter but did agree generally that they should not release aspects of the story that they had been made aware of during DoD early notification and which did not appear in the stories already out or in preparation; nor should this privy information be used to confirm speculation concerning an operation.

5. In this connection, the media generally did not agree with a view voiced by some members of the panel that, absolutely to guarantee security, pool notification would not be made until the first military personnel had hit the beach or airhead even though advance military preparation could speed the poolers to the site in the least time possible. The panel did not take a position on this, but some felt that carefully planned pool transportation could meet the media's objections in many, possibly most, cases. For example, in remote areas the pool could be assembled in a location close to the operation using overseas correspondents who

would not have to travel from the United States. This is a subject worthy of detailed discussion in the military-media meetings proposed in Recommendation 8a.

6. In this connection, the panel recognized that in many areas of the world an established press presence would be encountered by U.S. forces irrespective of a decision as to whether or not a pool would be used. This consideration would have to be included in initial public affairs planning.

7. There was no unanimity among the media representatives as to whether correspondents, pooled or otherwise, should be in the "first wave" or any other precise point in the operation. All did agree that media presence should be as soon as possible and feasible. The panel believes that such timing has to be decided on a case-by-case basis.

8. Neither the media nor the panel agreed on use in a pool of full-time media employees who are not U.S. citizens. The media tended to agree that, if the parent organization considered such employees reliable, they should be allowed to be pool members. Based on public experience in Vietnam, there were many cases where such employees proved entirely reliable; however, some did not. The panel suggests that this has to be another case-by-case situation.

9. There was also a divergence of opinion among the media as to what news organizations should make up a pool, although all agreed that the most important criterion was probably which organizations cover the widest American audience. Several media representatives suggested specific media pools, but, unfortunately, they varied widely. The panel was not in full agreement on this subject either, but did agree that the following types of news organizations should have top priority. The panel further agreed that DoD should take the factors discussed in this paragraph into account when designating news organizations to participate in a pool.

a. Wire services. AP and UPI to have priority. A reporter from each and a photographer from either one should be adequate. In a crash situation where inadequate planning time has been available, a reporter from one wire service and a photographer from the other could provide a two-person pool.

b. Television. A two-person TV pool (one correspondent, one film/sound man) can do the job for a brief time although perhaps minimally. All TV representatives agreed that a three-person team is better and can do more. A panel suggestion that a six-person team (one cameraman, one sound man, and one reporter each from ABC, CBS, NBC, and CNN) seemed agreeable to the four networks although the load on the two technicians would be difficult to handle. The panel has no suggestion on this except that TV pool representatives must have high priority with two representatives as the minimum and augmentation to depend on space available. This should be a matter of discussion at the meetings suggested in Recommendation 8a. The question of radio participation in pools must also be resolved.

c. News Magazines. One reporter and one color photographer.

d. Daily newspapers. At least one reporter. The panel agreed with newspaper representatives that, although newspapers do use wire service copy and photos, at least one newspaper pooler is needed for the special aspects of newspaper coverage not provided by the wire services. Criteria suggested for use when deciding which newspaper(s) to include in a pool included: Circulation, whether the newspaper has a news service, does the newspaper specialize in military and foreign affairs, and does it cover the Pentagon regularly. There was some agreement among the media representatives that there are probably not more than 8-10 newspapers which should be considered for pooling under these criteria.

10. In addition to the type of embargo necessary when a pooling news agency is notified in advance about a military operation (i.e., nothing to be said about it until it begins) there is another type applicable to some military operations. This second type was used with great success in Vietnam and restricts media accompanying the forces from filing or releasing any information about the progress of the operation until the on-scene commander determines that such release will not impair his security by informing the opposing commander about his objectives. Normally, this is not a problem as general objectives quickly become apparent. In the case of a special objective, there might be some delay in authorizing stories until either the objective is attained or it is obvious the enemy commander knows what it is. In any case, this type of embargo is an option to planners that the media would almost certainly accept as opposed to not having correspondents with the forces from the outset or close to it. The panel did not have a consensus on this matter.

11. Media representatives emphasized the readiness of correspondents to accept, as in the past, the physical dangers inherent in military operations and agreed that the personal security of correspondents should not be a factor in planning media participation in military operations.

Recommendation 3:

In connection with the use of pools, the Joint Chiefs of Staff recommend to the Secretary of Defense that he study the matter of whether to use a pre-established and constantly updated accreditation or notification list of correspondents in case of a military operation for which a pool is required or just the establishment of a news agency list for use in the same circumstances.

Comments

1. The panel envisions that in either case the agency would select the individual(s) to be its representatives in the pool. In the case of the ac-creditation/notification list, there would presumably be several names from each news agency/organization to provide the necessary flexibili-ty. The agency would have provided the names in advance to DoD. In the case of the news agency/organization list, DoD would decide which agencies would be in the pool and the agencies would pick the person(s) desired without reference to a list. There was no agreement as to whether DoD should have approval authority of the individuals named to be pool members. The media representatives were unanimously against such ap-proval as were some members of the panel. However, other panel members believed that in the case of an extremely sensitive operation, DoD should have such authority.

2. There was no agreement among either those who appeared before the panel or among the panel itself on this matter. More in both groups seemed to favor simply establishing a news agency list including wire services, television, news magazines and newspapers from which to pick when DoD establishes a pool.

3. This particular problem is one that should be resolved in advance of a military operation and should be a subject of discussion in connec-tion with the military-media meetings suggested in Recommendation 8a.

4. This recommendation does not concern the accreditation that would have to be given each correspondent covering an operation, either at first or later, by the senior on-site commander. Traditionally, this ac-creditation is limited to establishing that the individual is a bona fide reporter (represents an actual media organization).

Recommendation 4:

That a basic tenet governing media access to military operations should be voluntary compliance by the media with security guidelines or ground rules established and issued by the military. These rules should be as few as possible and should be worked out during the planning process for each operation. Violations would mean exclusion of the correspondent(s) concerned from further coverage of the operation.

Comments

1. The media were in support of this concept as opposed to formal censorship of any type, and all media representatives agreed that their organizations would abide by these ground rules. This agreement would place a heavy responsibility on the news media to exercise care so as not to inadvertently jeopardize mission security or troop safety.

2. The guidelines/ground rules are envisioned to be similar to those used in Vietnam. . . . Recognizing that each situation will be different, public affairs planners would use the Vietnam rules as a starting point, as they were worked out empirically during Vietnam by public affairs and security personnel and, for the most part, in cooperation with news media on the scene. All media representatives who addressed the issue agreed that the ground rules worked out satisfactorily in Vietnam.

Recommendation 5:
Public affairs planning for military operations should include sufficient equipment and qualified military personnel whose function is to assist correspondents in covering the operation adequately.

Comments

1. The military personnel referred to in this recommendation are normally called escorts; however, this term has developed some unfortunate connotations as far as the media are concerned. In any case, the panel's recommendation is designed to provide personnel who, acting as agents of the on-scene commander, will perform such functions as keep the correspondents abreast of the situation; arrange for interviews and briefings; arrange for their transportation to appropriate locations; ensure they are fed and housed, if necessary; and be as helpful as possible consistent with security and troop safety.

2. Almost all of the media representatives agreed that such escorts are desirable, especially at the beginning of an operation, to assist in media coverage. As the operation progresses and the reporters become familiar with what is going on, the media representatives were generally less enthusiastic about this type of assistance.

3. All the media were against escorts if their goal was to try to direct, censor, or slant coverage. However, most agreed that pointing out possible ground rule violations and security problems would be part of the escort's responsibility.

4. The point was made to the panel and the media representatives that escorts were often required in Vietnam, especially after about mid-1968, without many problems arising. One of the major advantages of escorts was making sure the reporters had a full and accurate understanding of the operation being covered.

5. The senior on-scene commander will decide how long escorting should continue after an operation begins.

Recommendation 6:
Planners should carefully consider media communications requirements to assure the earliest feasible availability. However, these communications must not interfere with combat and combat support operations. If necessary and feasible, plans should include communicative facilities dedicated to the news media.

Comments

1. Media representatives were unanimous in preferring provision for use of their own communications or using local civilian communications when possible. They were also unanimous, however, in the need for access to military communications if nothing else were available, especially in the opening stages of an operation.

2. Permitting media coverage without providing some sort of filing capability does not make sense unless an embargo is in force.

3. Although not discussed in depth during the panel meetings, communications availability is an obvious factor in determining press pool size. Planners should consider the varying deadlines of the different types of media. For example, newsmagazine reporters usually have more time to file thus permitting courier service as a possible satisfactory solution from their standpoint.

4. There was considerable discussion of the possibility of media-provided satellite uplinks being a future threat to security if technology permits real-time or near real-time copy and film/tape processing. The media representatives felt that such a possibility was not imminent; however, the discussions resulted in Recommendation 8d being in-

cluded in the report. One panel member made the point that such real-time or near real-time capability has long existed for radio news including the Murrow reporting during World War II.

Recommendation 7:

Planning factors should include provision for intra- and inter-theater transportation support of the media. There was no panel comment on this matter.

Recommendation 8:

To improve media-military understanding and cooperation:

a. CJCS should recommend to the Secretary of Defense that a program be undertaken by ASD(PA) for top military public affairs representatives to meet with news organization leadership, to include meetings with individual news organizations, on a reasonably regular basis to discuss mutual problems, including relationships with the media during military operations and exercises. This program should begin as soon as possible.

b. Enlarge programs already underway to improve military understanding of the media via public affairs instruction in service schools and colleges, to include media participation when possible.

c. Seek improved media understanding of the military through more visits by commanders and line officers to news organizations.

d. CJCS should recommend that the Secretary of Defense host at an early date a working meeting with representatives of the broadcast news media to explore the special problems of ensuring military security when and if there is real-time news media audiovisual coverage of a battlefield and, if special problems exist, how they can best be dealt with consistent with the basic principle set forth at the beginning of this section of the report.

Comments

1. The panel became convinced during its meetings with both media and military representatives that any current actual or perceived lack of mutual understanding and cooperation could be largely eliminated through the time-tested vehicle of having reasonable people sit down with reasonable people and discuss their problems. Although some of this has occurred from time to time through the years, there has not been enough, especially in recent years. The panel envisages that these meetings would be between ASD(PA) and/or his representatives and the

senior leadership of both media umbrella organizations and individual major news organizations. A number of media representatives appearing before the panel said that they thought the media would be happy to participate in such a program. The program should include use of the Chiefs/Directors of Public Affairs of the Services, some of whom are already doing this.

2. Such meetings would provide an excellent opportunity to discuss problems or potential problems involving future military operations/exercises such as pooling, security and troop safety, accreditation, logistic support, and, most importantly, improving mutual respect, trust, understanding, and cooperation in general.

3. The panel does not exclude any news organizations in this recommendation, but practicality will lead to emphasis on meetings with major organizations. It would be equally useful for commanders in the field and their public affairs officers to conduct similar meetings with local and regional media in their areas, some of which are also underway at this time.

4. Both the panel and the media representatives lauded the efforts underway today to reinsert meaningful public affairs instruction in service schools and colleges. Many officers are sheltered from becoming involved with the news media until they are promoted to certain assignments where they suddenly come face-to-face with the media. If they have not been adequately informed in advance of the mutual [sic] with each other, they sometimes tend to make inadequate decisions concerning media matters. In this connection, several media representatives told the panel they would be, and in some cases have already been, delighted to cooperate in this process by talking to classes and seminars.

5. Several media representatives also were enthusiastic about undertaking an effort to inform their employees about the military, primarily through visits of commanders and other appropriate personnel to their headquarters or elsewhere in their organizations. It was also apparent that some media are concerned with this problem to the point that they are taking an introspective look at their relations not only with the military but other institutions.

General Comments

1. The panel agreed that public affairs planning for military operations involving allied forces should also consider making plans flexible enough to cover allied media participation, even in pools in some cases.

2. It was pointed out to the panel and should be noted that planners may also have to consider the desires of U.S. Ambassadors and their country teams when operations take place in friendly foreign countries. Some of these problems can, of course, be handled by the commanders and senior public affairs personnel on the scene, but they should be alerted to them in advance.

3. The media representatives all agreed that U.S. media should have first priority in covering U.S. military operations. The panel generally agreed that this must be handled on a case-by-case basis, especially when allied forces are involved.

Final Comment

An adversarial—perhaps politely critical would be a better term—relationship between the media and the government, including the military, is healthy and helps guarantee that both institutions do a good job. However, this relationship must not become antagonistic—an "us versus them" relationship. The appropriate media role in relation to the government has been summarized aptly as being neither that of a lap dog nor an attack dog but, rather, a watch dog. Mutual antagonism and distrust are not in the best interests of the media, the military, or the American people.

In the final analysis, no statement of principles, policies, or procedures, no matter how carefully crafted, can guarantee the desired results because they have to be carried out by people—the people in the military and the people in the media. So, it is the good will of the people involved, their spirit, their genuine efforts to do the job for the benefit of the United States, on which a civil and fruitful relationship hinges.

The panel believes that, if its recommendations are adopted, and the people involved are infused with the proper spirit, the twin imperatives of genuine mission security/troop safety on the one hand and a free flow of information to the American public on the other will be achieved.

In other words, the optimum solution to ensure proper media coverage of military operations will be to have the military—represented by competent, professional public affairs personnel and commanders who understand media problems—working with the media—represented by competent, professional reporters and editors who understand military problems—in a nonantagonistic atmosphere. The panel urges both institutions to adopt this philosophy and make it work.

Winant Sidle
Major General, USA, Retired
Chairman